South Africa:
In Transition
to What?

THE WASHINGTON PAPERS

... intended to meet the need for an authoritative, yet prompt, public appraisal of the major developments in world affairs.

President, CSIS: David M. Abshire

Series Editor: Walter Laqueur

Director of Publications: Nancy B. Eddy

Managing Editor: Donna R. Spitler

MANUSCRIPT SUBMISSION

The Washington Papers and Praeger Publishers welcome inquiries concerning manuscript submissions. Please include with your inquiry a curriculum vitae, synopsis, table of contents, and estimated manuscript length. Manuscripts must be between 120–200 double-spaced typed pages. All submissions will be peer reviewed. Submissions to *The Washington Papers* should be sent to *The Washington Papers*; The Center for Strategic and International Studies; 1800 K Street NW; Suite 400; Washington, DC 20006. Book proposals should be sent to Praeger Publishers; One Madison Avenue; New York NY 10010.

The Washington Papers/132

South Africa: In Transition to What?

Helen Kitchen, Editor

Published with The Center for
Strategic and International Studies
Washington, D.C.

PRAEGER

New York
Westport, Connecticut
London

Library of Congress Cataloging-in-Publication Data

South Africa, in transition to what?

  (The Washington papers, ISSN 0278-937X ; 132)
  Includes index.
  1. South Africa – Politics and government –
1978–   . I. Kitchen, Helen A. II. Series.
DT779.952.S654 1988   968.06′3   87-35918
ISBN 0-275-92975-2 (alk. paper)
ISBN 0-275-92974-4 (pbk. : alk. paper)

The *Washington Papers* are written under the auspices of The Center
for Strategic and International Studies (CSIS) and published
with CSIS by Praeger Publishers. The views expressed in these papers
are those of the authors and not necessarily those of the Center.

Library of Congress Catalog Card Number: 87-35918
ISBN: 0-275-92975-2 (cloth)
     0-275-92974-4 (paper)

First published in 1988

Praeger Publishers, One Madison Avenue, New York, NY 10010
A division of Greenwood Press, Inc.

Printed in the United States of America

∞

The paper used in this book complies with the Permanent
Paper Standard issued by the National Information Standards
Organization (Z39.48-1984).

10 9 8 7 6 5 4 3 2 1

Contents

Foreword

South Africa is clearly a country in transition—but in transition to what? Analysts (as well as advocates across the racial, political, economic, and ideological spectrum) are becoming increasingly cautious in their citations of analogies and their predictions of this divided nation's destiny.

Each of the chapters in this book focuses on specific segments of the jigsaw puzzle from which South Africa's future, for better or worse, will be assembled. The authors come from a range of geographical and professional bases, but meet one imperative qualification: residence or repeated physical presence in South Africa. We are looking here through prisms focused on the whys and wherefores of South Africa as seen from within.

Although none of the chapters address directly the issue of United States policy, one of the objectives of publishing this particular collection is to impress upon readers (especially Americans) that the South Africa that emerges from today's strife will be primarily determined by internal factors. Evidence has accumulated over the past two years that Eminent Persons interlocutors, "constructive engagement," distinguished Advisory Committees, made-in-Washington "comprehensive" anti-apartheid legislation, disinvestment, selective economic and diplomatic sanctions by

European trading partners, Sullivan principles, expanding support of black education programs, and other externally devised initiatives can affect but not mandate how or whether South Africa's fractured society can find a way to avoid a lemmings scenario.

The American inclination to address South Africa (among other issues) as "a problem to be solved" runs the risk of oversimplifying both dynamics and personalities. South Africa is more than a morality play. It is one of the world's most complex societies, and becoming more so every day. It is our first responsibility to get to know its many dimensions better.

Each of the chapters in this volume, except for Zwelakhe Sisulu's, was previously published as an issue of *CSIS Africa Notes* — a briefing paper series launched by the African Studies Program in 1982 to "serve the special needs of decision makers and analysts with Africa-related responsibilities in governments, corporations, the media, research institutions, universities, and other arenas." Each chapter is datelined, to emphasize that this is how the situation, event, or issue being addressed appeared through a particular set of lenses at a particular time in what is likely to be a prolonged transition.

Helen Kitchen
Director of African Studies
Center for Strategic and International Studies

October 1987

Contributors to This Volume

Heribert Adam, a professor of sociology at Simon Fraser University in Vancouver, British Columbia, spent his 1986–1987 sabbatical serving as director of the Center for Intergroup Studies at the University of Cape Town. He has also studied and taught in Germany. Dr. Adam's many publications include *South Africa without Apartheid*, coauthored with his wife, Kogila Moodley (University of California Press, 1986); *Ethnic Power Mobilized*, coauthored with Hermann Giliomee (Yale University Press, 1979); and *Modernizing Racial Domination* (University of California Press, 1971).

William J. Foltz is professor of political science at Yale University, director of Yale's Center for International and Area Studies, and associate director of the Yale-Wesleyan Southern Africa Research Project. His many publications on Africa include *From French West Africa to the Mali Federation* (Yale University Press, 1965); *Resolving Conflict in Africa*, coauthor (Yale University Press, 1970); *Elite Opinion on United States Policy Toward Africa* (Council on Foreign Relations, 1979); *Arms and the African: Military Influences on Africa's International Relations*, coedited with Henry Bienen (Yale University Press, 1985); and chapters in more than a dozen other books.

John A. Marcum is author of the classic two-volume work, *The Angolan Revolution – The Anatomy of an Explosion (1950–1962)* (MIT Press, 1969) and *Exile Politics and Guerrilla Warfare (1962–1976)* (MIT Press, 1978). His other major publications include *Education, Race, and Social Change in South Africa* (University of California Press, 1982). Dr. Marcum, coordinator of international programs and professor of politics at the University of California at Santa Cruz, is a former president of the 2,000-member African Studies Association and frequently travels to southern Africa.

Steven McDonald received his Master's degree in African politics from the School of Oriental and African Studies, University of London. He began his professional career as an aide to Senator Stuart Symington of Missouri, and subsequently served in a range of African posts as a career Foreign Service officer in the Department of State (1970–1979). From 1982 until 1985, he was executive director of the United States–South Africa Leader Exchange Program (USSALEP).

Ken Owen is editor of *Business Day* (Johannesburg). From 1969 to 1977, he was Washington bureau chief for the Argus group of South African newspapers and subsequently served (1982–1985) as editor of the *Sunday Express* (Johannesburg).

Robert I. Rotberg, a frequent visitor to southern Africa, is academic vice president of Tufts University. His many writings include *South Africa and Its Neighbors: Regional Security and Self-Interest*, coauthor (Lexington Books, D.C. Heath and Company, 1985); *Namibia: Political and Economic Prospects*, ed. (Lexington Books, D.C. Heath and Company, 1983); *Suffer the Future: Policy Choices in Southern Africa* (Harvard University Press, 1980); *Black Heart: Gore-Browne and the Politics of Multiracial Zambia* (University of California Press, 1978); and *The Rise of Nationalism in Central Africa* (Harvard University Press, 1965).

Zwelakhe Sisulu was editor of the *New Nation*, a news-

paper published under the auspices of the Catholic Bishops'
Conference, from 1985 until he was detained without
charges under South Africa's state of emergency in July
1986. Born in Soweto (the son of Walter Sisulu, an ANC
leader sentenced to life imprisonment along with Nelson
Mandela in 1964), Mr. Sisulu was educated in the township
and later in Swaziland. In 1975, he became one of the first
blacks to be accepted for the South African Associated
Newspapers (SAAN) journalism cadet course and subsequently served as news editor of the *Sunday Post* and as
first president of what became the Media Workers' Association of South Africa (MWASA). He spent the academic year
1984–1985 as a Nieman Fellow in Journalism at Harvard
University. The chapter carrying his byline in this volume
is excerpted from his keynote address to an historic National Education Crisis Committee conference he helped to organize in Durban in March 1986.

Michael Spicer is public affairs advisor to the Anglo
American Corporation. He was formerly director of programs for the South African Institute of International Affairs, Johannesburg.

John de St. Jorre was born in London and educated in
England and Singapore. A former Africa and Middle East
correspondent of *The Observer* (London), he is author of
The Brothers' War: Biafra and Nigeria (Houghton Mifflin,
1972) and *A House Divided: South Africa's Uncertain Future* (Carnegie Endowment, 1977), and was a senior writer
for the Rockefeller Foundation-sponsored Study Commission on U.S. Policy toward Southern Africa's report, *South
Africa: Time Running Out* (University of California Press,
1981). In 1983–1984, he was a senior associate at the Carnegie Endowment for International Peace in Washington,
D.C., and in 1982–1983 was Africa director of the Washing-
ton-based International Reporting Information Systems
(IRIS). He is currently coordinating a new publication series on South Africa for the Ford Foundation. One of his
contributions to this volume (Chapter 11, "A Reporter's
Notebook") originally appeared in the South African maga-

zine *Leadership* and was subsequently published, with permission, in the *CSIS Africa Notes* briefing paper series.

Stanley Uys, former political editor of the *Sunday Times* (Johannesburg) and now coeditor of the London-based monthly *Front File,* wrote his contribution to this volume while serving as London bureau chief for Times Media Ltd., publishers of the *Cape Times*, *Business Day*, the *Sunday Times*, and other leading English-language South African newspapers.

South Africa: In Transition to What?

1

South Africa: What Kind of Change?

William J. Foltz

November 1982

Discussion of the prospects for "meaningful" or "significant" change in South Africa has engaged Marxist, liberal, and conservative scholars for years. Like other participants in this perennial debate, I have tripped over my own predictions often enough to have bruised my *hubris*. I am afraid that I must disappoint anyone who wants a firm schedule and route map as to where South Africa goes from here. This does not imply that important changes are not taking place in South Africa. Indeed, some of the changes that have occurred or become apparent in the last seven years have been momentous, and at the least they allow us to exclude some possibilities for the future. There are, however, simply too many uncontrolled variables in the South African equation to permit anyone whose vision is not armed with perfect faith to predict the future with any degree of confidence.

The past year has been a momentous one in South Africa, marked in particular by the open split within the political ranks of Afrikanerdom and the formal announcement of plans to give Coloureds and Indians some representation in government. In political terms, the government has progressed almost to the stage it had reached prior to 1948. But this shift is based on a cumulation of social and eco-

1

nomic trends that make South African society today very different from what it was in 1948 when the National Party first came to power.

The demographic changes are perhaps most important. Since 1948 the white population has declined from almost one-quarter of the total to about 15 percent, and it likely will account for no more than 12 percent by the end of the century. The white population has also undergone major qualitative changes which have most greatly affected its Afrikaans-speaking portion. The modal Afrikaner is no longer a bible-toting, ill-educated boer; he is a middle-class civil servant living in a suburban split-level home, whose most immediate worries concern balancing installment payments on his color television, his new car, and the electronic burglar alarm system he has just installed. Thanks in large part to the electoral success of 1948, his ethnic community has now produced a substantial entrepreneurial and managerial class which has challenged the English-speaking community for control over the economy and which is now busy integrating itself with that community. In 1948 the income ratio between Afrikaners and English was 1 : 2, it is now about 1 : 1.3, and in urban areas it is nearly 1 : 1.

The African population has also changed substantially. Despite the fictions of grand apartheid, more than half the African population lives in "white" areas, and by the end of the century 60 percent of the total African population is expected to be urban. While African education and income have been scandalously repressed, both are increasing at a greater rate than is true for the white community. South African planning is now based on the assumption that by the end of the 1980s the majority of those completing secondary school will be Africans.

These demographic changes reflect and influence the evolution of the South African economy. The economy has moved through classic stages from one based predominantly on farming, to mining, to labor-intensive manufacturing, to one which is now increasingly capital-intensive. The leading sectors of the South African economy, including the most recently developed mining operations, are capital-intensive and thus require a skilled labor force. The demographic changes dictate that this labor force be increasingly black, and that much of black labor be permanently and stably settled, educated, and organized. This does not require, it must be noted, that all, or even the majority, of blacks be included in this advanced sector of the labor force, only that much of that sector be black. Thus the black homelands need no longer function to provide a reserve army of the unemployed to hold down wage rates in unskilled occupations; rather, they are becoming dumping grounds for unskilled surplus labor no longer needed by the dominant economy. Blacks have another key role to play in the emerging South African economy. They are consumers of the goods that economy produces, and the importance of that market is attested to by the vigor with which its tastes are being prospected by South African industry and market research organizations.

The last few years have seen a new relationship develop between government and private industry. Although South African big business remains to the left of government on racial issues, the old antagonism between the English/Jewish-dominated private sector and the Afrikaner-dominated public sector has been greatly attenuated. Government and industry see themselves, somewhat reluctantly, as partners in a joint task of technocratic modernization of the country. In this partnership, industry sometimes takes on quasi-governmental functions (the Urban Foundation, for example), while government has reciprocated in selling off parts of the large state-owned industrial sector to private industry.

Political change in the southern Africa region – the coming to power of black governments in the neighborhood – is another underlying trend affecting change in South Africa. The most immediate effect of this change was economic: it ended the "Outward Policy" of the early Vorster years, which looked for the rapid expansion of markets in Africa for fairly unsophisticated South African manufactures which might have allowed South Africa to continue to rely on an unskilled and miserably paid work force of migrant blacks. The political effects are no less important. The shock of Robert Mugabe's electoral victory in Zimbabwe in 1980 still reverberates through white opinion and unquestionably has raised black spirits and confidence within the Republic. In the short run, Mugabe's victory has strengthened the South African government's intransigence and undercut its willingness to compromise in Namibia and to negotiate openly with potentially cooperative black leaders such as Chief Mangosuthu G. Buthelezi and Dr. Nthato Motlana. The white population has furthermore been augmented by the addition of highly conservative, but non-Afrikaner, immigrants from Mozambique, Angola, and Zimbabwe who will be joining the electorate in significant numbers over the next few years.

The augmented sense of threat and isolation, ritualized in the slogan "Total Onslaught," has assisted (and been promoted by) the rise of the military to a key position of influence in the government. The accession of P.W. Botha to the prime ministership has brought General Magnus Malan's military to replace H.J. van den Bergh's Bureau of State Security as the principal adjunct to state power, if not the power behind the throne. The military's influence within the government complements the increased influence within the prime minister's office of comparatively young and well-educated technocrats, mostly Afrikaners, whose loyalty is to the state rather than to any particular ideological or ethnic identity, and who deal on easy and equal terms with their counterparts in the private sector.

As a result of these long-term trends and of the increased pressures on South Africa, Vorster and particularly Botha have worked to construct a modern state apparatus. Although that apparatus is riven with the same cleavages that affect the white electorate and is less responsive to government initiative than many would wish, there can be little doubt that its absolute level of power has increased. Nevertheless, given the external and internal challenges the South African system faces, the ability of the government to do much with that power is probably decreasing.

Black Politics

In at least one sense, African politics in South Africa has also returned to the status quo ante 1948: The African National Congress (ANC) has been reestablished as the leading organization providing symbolic expression of black aspirations. Recent opinion polls confirm the casual impression that the ANC has substantially increased its audience at the expense of the Pan-Africanist Congress (PAC), Inkatha, AZAPO, and various forms of Black Consciousness. Various recent polls show that the imprisoned Nelson Mandela remains the most frequent choice of the urban African population as the leader who comes closest to representing people's aspirations. Even aside from the imprecision and transitory nature of opinions expressed to pollsters, this endorsement should be viewed with caution. Mandela has become a mythical figure during his years on Robben Island whose understandable popularity (like that of Kenya's Jomo Kenyatta in the 1950s) is aided by his inability to do anything that might put it to the test.

Nor does this popularity necessarily rub off on leaders of the exile wing of the ANC. There is little evidence that formal ANC ideology plays a major role in that organization's appeal, although its emphatic opposition to the country's division into ethnic homelands has widespread support. Rather, the ANC's popularity appears to rest principally on its role of systematically rejecting the South African system and on the symbolic importance of its sabotage and assassination campaign as tangible evidence of that rejection. The ANC's campaign of selective violence is an important recruiting and morale-boosting device. Although ANC acts of violence have steadily increased over the last three years, they have not yet reached the point where large numbers of blacks are obliged to pay a price for them in police repression. When that occurs, the ANC's popularity will be put to a new test, a test the government seems to want to avoid.

Trade unions represent the most dynamic sector of Af-

rican organization within South Africa and are a direct response to the changing nature and needs of the South African economy, and to African initiative as expressed notably
in the Durban strikes of 1973. As yet, the trade union
movement includes some 10–12 percent of the nonagri-
cultural African labor force, but it speaks for many more. It
is not an integrated movement – far from it – and individual
unions' relationship with political movements like the ANC
varies from clandestine cooperation to overt hostility. Despite their highly decentralized and fledgling nature, the
trade unions represent the only formal, legal, and above-
ground demand organizations for blacks with which the
state and private industry must contend. For their own
thoroughly capitalist purposes, the most dynamic sectors
of industry have welcomed and even fostered the growth of
unions, in some cases forcing government's hand; even the
mining industry seems likely to accept black unionization.
The state apparatus is badly divided on how to treat unions
(and frequently enough treats them with brutal stupidity),
but the economic and international costs of generalized repression would now be such that the government would be
unlikely to undertake such a policy in the absence of a
major crisis.

The trade union movement has concentrated on trade-
union issues narrowly defined; these are extended at most
(as in the Eastern Cape) to include some local issues of
community organization. Neither from the trade unions nor
from any other base has any clear leader or group of leaders
emerged to speak confidently in the name of a broad cross-
section of black opinion. Buthelezi may come closest to
this, but it is increasingly apparent that his support rests
on and is limited by his control over KwaZulu. The government has gone out of its way to undercut his attempts to
appeal to a wider constituency and may yet succeed in de-
stroying his base in his home territory. Other leaders attain
prominence as spokesmen for particular grievances (the
Committee of Ten, for example), but they are captives of
these grievances and lack the political resources to shape
and mobilize opinion and to create loyal followings. In

short, they cannot really lead, nor are they able to form more than transitory, tactical alliances with other "leaders."

This leadership vacuum does not completely redound to the benefit of a government seeking some form of stable accommodation with blacks. The South African government has clearly lost whatever ideological or psychological hegemony it may once have had over blacks. At best it can coerce a sullen compliance. To get more, it will have to risk allowing real leaders to emerge and to deploy real political resources. This is a step which the government is still far from willing to contemplate seriously.

Formal government policy toward Africans has undergone very little change in its broadest outlines. P.W. Botha appears to be still bent on implementing grand apartheid under the guise of the Constellation of Southern African States (hence the pressures on Swaziland and Lesotho and the preference for an internal settlement in Namibia), with a more limited Confederation of (white) South Africa and the homelands as a fallback. Domestically, the government hopes to create a reasonably stable, basically urban African work force led by a collaborating middle class (hence the "Orderly Movement and Settlement of Black Persons" bill). But government action and resources, both for coercion and inducement, are incommensurate with the aims. Hence the overall paralysis of political initiative toward Africans that has afflicted South African governments since the Soweto uprisings in 1976.

White Politics

In 1982 the South African government faced two major substantive decisions—internal constitutional reordering with a limited political role for Coloureds and Indians, and acquiescence in a Namibia settlement—and faced them in dispersed array. The May 1981 elections resulted in a comparatively poor showing for the ruling National Party, which suffered significant disaffection from Afrikaner voters to the right, especially in the Transvaal, and some loss to the Progressive Federal Party (PFP) on the left. Overall electoral participation continued its decline from 80 percent 15 years ago to 65 percent. The formal split came in February 1982 over the symbolic issue of "healthy power sharing" with Coloureds and Indians, in effect the implementation of decisions taken by the National Party back in 1977. Although P.W. Botha retained leadership of the party and freed himself from having to face the *verkrampte* carping of Andries Treurnicht in the parliamentary caucus, he won out only thanks to the support of the conservative Transvaal "centrists" led by F.W. de Klerk—not a group likely to approve bold new reforms.

The name of the new right-wing opposition party tells us much about the new face of white South African politics. It is the "Conservative Party," a name which contains no ethnic overtones. It appeals to conservative English-speaking voters (especially in Natal), to the new immigrants, and above all to the lower- and middle-level Afrikaner civil servants in their suburban split-levels. It projects an image of stolid social respectability and leaves to the Herstigte Nasionale Party (HNP) the vulgar racial appeals to the Afrikaner and Portuguese working class. This division of clientele, as much as leadership rivalry, has kept the right-wing opposition from merging, or even developing an electoral nonaggression pact. The political divisions have seriously affected Afrikanerdom and have repercussions through most of the parallel cultural, religious, and professional organizations, including the press and the Afrikaner Broederbond. With the National Party itself divided into several ideological (or at least programmatic) factions, and with Afrikaner intellectuals now leading the PFP, ethnic unity appears to be a thing of the past.

The National Party's poor showing in the August 1982 by-election appears to have convinced Botha that he could take on only one contentious decision. Unfortunately, he chose to proceed with domestic "power sharing" and to put Namibia on the shelf. I say unfortunately, because there is very much less here than meets Dr. Treurnicht's eye. It is not at all clear that the Coloureds, at least, will support the proposal or for very long back up any leader who does. It does seem very clear, however, that fairly little real power will be shared under the new "dispensation" and that the framework is not one that can practically be extended some day to include Africans. More important than the power-sharing provision is the power-concentrating effect of the proposal, which would create an executive largely independent of parliament and capable of ruling through an increasingly centralized state apparatus. It is this latter aspect of the proposal which has aroused greatest concern within the professional ranks of the National Party, and it is not yet clear that Botha and his technocratic senior civil servants, supported in this by much of the business community, will end up having their way.

The factionalism in the Afrikaner community returns Afrikaner politics to its normal state prior to 1948. It is in large part a consequence, however, of the great success of 1948, which allowed Afrikaners to use the state to promote members of their community to leading positions throughout South African society, particularly in business. The Afrikaner community is now riven with the class, institutional, and intellectual divisions that are the normal lot of mankind in industrial society. Rather than coming together under pressure from their own black population and a largely hostile world, the Afrikaners are fragmenting, with each group seeking its own vision of security and immediate self-interest.

"Violent Evolution"

Where does all this leave the prospects of change? First, we can say with some confidence that South Africa is not on the verge of imminent revolution. The government's repressive apparatus is too effective; the military has too much sway over neighboring states; the divisions within the white population do not yet seriously undermine the consensus on the necessity for white political domination; and above all the black population lacks access to the resources

that might permit effective leadership to arise. Black grievances are such that the country may be in a "prerevolutionary situation," but it has been there for a long while.

Increasingly, South Africa is becoming what many
Marxist writers have wrongly claimed it has been all
along—a system of rule by big business in alliance with the
military and state sector technocrats. This development
has produced new cleavages in the white population and
will increasingly shift the ideological basis for repressive
rule from crass racism to a rationale based on technocratic
efficiency. This will permit many of the daily humiliations
of petty apartheid to fall by the wayside but will not seriously undermine the willingness of whites to defend their
privileges.

Although class divisions within white society are becoming increasingly important politically, South Africa is
far from providing conditions for a classic class struggle.
Race is much too powerful a crosscutting cleavage in South
Africa, not because it evokes primordial prejudices, but because for whites, and many Coloureds and Indians, it is
linked to real material interests.

If blacks lack the resources to force revolutionary
change, the white government lacks the power, the vision,
and the will to do what would be necessary to bring about
peaceful progress. Minimum requirements for such progress would include drastic modifications in the homeland
system, including very large economic transfers to build up
the black rural economy, and above all allowing a black
middle class to develop independent political resources.
Even though a few persons in government circles see the
problem in those terms, they are politically hamstrung by
the workings of South Africa's peculiar white democratic
system and by deep divisions within the state apparatus.
If the South African political system has not yet enthusi-
astically co-opted a Buthelezi, a Motlana, a Percy Qoboza,
it has little hope of co-opting black leaders of the future, whatever constitutional rearrangements it may
produce.

The policies of the great powers will play a role in

South Africa's future, but they seem likely to play that role largely by default. In the absence of dramatic regional events, the United States and the other Western nations will continue to deal with South Africa at arm's length, but deal with it nonetheless. The emergence of *any* internal, strong black leadership would evoke a positive response in Washington, but in the absence of such leadership U.S. policy innovations will mostly continue to come as a reaction to violent episodes within South Africa. The Soviet Union's principal role for the moment seems to be that of useful support for the South African regime's "total onslaught" ideology. (Just as South Africa provides helpful support for Moscow's policy in the rest of Africa.) Although the Soviet Union will certainly continue to aid the ANC's political and military efforts, it shows no sign of willingness to risk any direct involvement in the struggle or to use its own production of gold and other minerals to bring pressure on the South African economy. In the absence of more positive external involvement, the most important sources of change will be internal to South Africa.

Change in South Africa will most likely continue to occur in a discontinuous, sometimes violent, manner, which will satisfy few. Initially at least, interactions between trade unions, industry, and the government will be keys to the pattern of change. They are most likely to proceed (and in the process to increase the status and material welfare of many blacks) according to what former U.S. Ambassador to South Africa William Edmondson has aptly called "violent evolution." Over the next several years South Africa will change further, as the effects of underlying social, economic, and regional trends continue to work themselves out. These in time will force a divided white population and the government into new attempts at political accommodation with the black majority. Nothing in the present situation suggests that those attempts will succeed until black leaders acquire the resources for independent political organization and action. When they do, the pattern of accommodation that emerges will likely bear little relation to anyone's current projections.

2

The Process of Decision Making in Contemporary South Africa

Robert I. Rotberg

December 1983

Before 1980, especially during the 12-year prime ministership of Balthazar Johannes Vorster, the South African
government's decision-making process was less than methodical. Although rigid in personality and an unquestioned, authoritarian leader, Vorster believed in a decentralized style of management. Cabinet ministers conformed to
the overall policies that were set by Vorster and a small
oligarchy. But within that conformity to an overall plan,
the ministers were encouraged to run their departments
with little interference from the prime minister. Such autonomy stimulated political competition among departments. Often ministries were kept ignorant of what others
were doing or planning. Collective responsibility was difficult to impose. In practice, there were no instruments, other than personal appeals to the prime minister, to limit this
competition or to coordinate the different, sometimes
crosscutting, governmental activities.

Vorster, like Hendrik F. Verwoerd before him, may have
welcomed such rivalries. But it is more likely that the absence of coordination and the untidy administrative style
were carried over from earlier times, when the meshing of
the initiatives of one or more departments may have been
less critical to the functioning of the state.

For Vorster and his predecessors, informal methods

by and large produced sufficient results. Furthermore, a decentralized state mechanism accentuated the personal power of the prime minister, backed as he would have been by personal alliances, party prerogatives, and largely unchallenged control over the distribution of patronage and preferment. In a regimented society with common political goals, represented by an unadventuresome party caucus and held together by the imposition of discipline from the Broederbond and an allied church, the government functioned naturally as an assemblage of personalized and well-demarcated satrapies.

In Vorster's day, some of the departments (not the cabinet as a collectivity) were given (or demanded) command of the grand overarching policy initiatives of the state. The Bantu Administration Department (which later became Plural Relations and Development, and then Cooperation and Development) was charged with devising and overseeing the transformation of the Bantustans into quasi-autonomous homelands. The Information Department had its various forms of outreach and propaganda peddling, some clandestine and some not, and was almost immune from interference by Foreign Affairs. Finance operated largely on its own. So did Sport and other ministries, except when fundamental decisions had to be reached. At that point, either Vorster alone or Vorster and several cabinet and/or nongovernmental colleagues arrived at decisions on the basis of information provided (depending on the issue) by single or competing departments, or by the state's security apparatus.

General Hendrik van den Bergh was Vorster's closest confidant and a devoted advisor from the days of their internment at Koffiefontein in World War II. Van den Bergh, a security policeman, fashioned the secret Republican Intelligence group out of the Security Police, which he headed, when Vorster was minister of justice under Prime Minister Verwoerd in the early 1960s. Republican Intelligence was created at a time when the African National Congress, the Pan-Africanist Congress, and the Communist Party had all been driven underground and were challenging the state with violence. There was an external threat, too, for the outside world was becoming more and more hostile. Thus, van den Bergh organized the Republican Intelligence to gather information at home and abroad, to engage where necessary in espionage, and to strengthen the hand of those, like Vorster, who were determined to outwit local and foreign rivals.

In 1969, the still-clandestine Republican Intelligence became the nucleus of the new Bureau of State Security (BOSS), a department of state. BOSS attempted with some success to usurp the prime functions of the security police and military intelligence. As security advisor to Vorster, van den Bergh had great organizational strengths to add to those which derived from their long friendship. He made much of these advantages, but he won few friends among the police or military (especially the latter, whose minister throughout this period was Pieter Willem Botha).

BOSS doubled in size during its first 10 years and van den Bergh exercised more informal power than most South Africans realized. Along with Cornelius (Connie) Mulder, who served at various times as minister of information, of interior, and of plural relations, he helped plan and implement a policy of reaching out to Africans, of trading with them, of bribing or compromising foreigners of all kinds, of working effectively with Israel, and (paradoxically) of reforming South Africa's overseas image while simultaneously countering dissent at home. Van den Bergh opposed the military on the efficacy of what would now be called destabilization, and particularly over the invasion of Angola in 1975.

Van den Bergh's decisive influence is now widely known. What is less fully appreciated, however, is the extent to which BOSS, under van den Bergh's direction, provided what limited machinery of coordination existed during the Vorster era. As rudimentary as was that structure, it was in many respects much more significant, even powerful, than the formal apparatus that now exists. Van den Bergh was the crisis manager. With Vorster's blessing, and presumably at his behest, he dealt with emergencies and coordinated responses. As those crises became more and more charged and frequent, van den Bergh and BOSS moved more and more toward the center of decision making. How smoothly crises were managed is another question. Van den Bergh was an autocrat and the building of a consensus was neither his talent nor his immediate responsibility. But he did compel the diverse tentacles of the state to come to grips with problems that overwhelmed individual departments and, at times, threatened to overwhelm the government as a whole.

Informal techniques, unclear accounting, and administrative obscurantism have their uses, especially when a modern nation attempts to gain what its leaders regard as just ends by questionable means, or by means that the public would question if it only knew. In the case of South Africa under Vorster, the lack of a centralized, formal mechanism of decision making facilitated the hodgepodge of covert activities that eventually brought Vorster (and van den Bergh and Mulder) into disrepute and ended their control of the government. The great affairs of state, it transpired, had been decided by cronies huddling together and writing directives on the backs of envelopes. The Infogate, or Muldergate, scandal brought new people to power. It also mandated the search for a new system of decision making that would, ideally, provide better and more comprehensive information to aid the making of rational choices, provide a means of organizing that information, and offer a framework for deciding which among the many questions should be given priority attention. If these various elements were effectively meshed, then the coordination of the implementation of the ultimate decisions would, it was thought, be made both more systematic and more logical than before.

Total Onslaught and Total Strategy

An alternative apparatus already existed. Following a set of recommendations made by Justice Potgieter in 1972, the Security, Intelligence, and State Security Council Act was passed in the same year. But the State Security Council (SSC) provided for in the act remained only one of 20 cabinet committees until 1979. Vorster paid these committees little attention, their meetings were irregular and infrequent, their agendas were uncirculated, and no minutes were kept. Nor were minutes kept of cabinet meetings.

When P.W. Botha became prime minister in 1978, he needed (not least for political reasons) to assert control over BOSS, over what remained of Mulder's empire, and over what he correctly regarded as an upper- and middle-level bureaucracy that might well be loyal to Vorster. The military had scores to settle, too. Since the invasion of Angola in 1975, if not before, its analysis of how best to deal with South Africa's enemies had been at variance with cabinet policy. Its leaders, and Botha, had wanted to take the war to the enemy. Influenced by Israeli strategic doctrine, and smarting from their enforced humiliation in Angola, they were anxious to take charge. Moreover, Botha and his military advisors had since 1966 been running the defense ministry in an orderly manner. Given his sense of managerial pride, his instincts as a party technocrat, and a degree of militaristic scorn for the slough into which the country had stumbled, it was predictable that the new prime minister would undertake to centralize, streamline, and reorient the decision-making machinery of the state.

Botha was the first prime minister to recognize publicly that revolution was a real possibility in South Africa. In order to implement an effective counterrevolutionary strategy, the state needed to function as a disciplined unit (to use a consciously military metaphor). "Total onslaught" quickly became the code name used by Botha, General Magnus Malan, and others from the military establishment to characterize the behavior of the Soviets, antiapartheid activists, and anyone else willing to support the African National Congress or other guerrilla movements perceived to be threatening to South Africa. Malan and the others described this assault on the nation as being not merely militaristic, but also political, diplomatic, religious, psycho-

logical, cultural, and social. Only a "total strategy" could meet the total onslaught, and coordination was a necessary component of the total response. Moreover, when a state is assaulted totally, everything with which the government might conceivably concern itself becomes a fit subject for concerned state study, analysis, and policy guidance.

There is a further consideration that may directly or indirectly have brought not only Botha but a range of other Afrikaner power-wielders to a recognition that some new method was necessary if apartheid were to continue to protect the *volk* in a changing and troubled world. Apartheid had begun to lose its internal legitimacy—what some have called its hegemonic character and appeal. (See Hermann Giliomee, *Parting of the Ways: South African Politics 1976–1982*, Cape Town: David Philip, 1982.) If so, or if the rethinking of the validity (as well as the efficacy) of radical discrimination and separate development by some Afrikaners (*verligte* ones, if that concept is helpful) had focused the prime minister's ideas, that line of analysis had also entered the military mind. The new ethic was one of survival through modernization, but not by challenging the very foundations of Afrikaner power. What Botha and officers alike chose as a means of countering the apartheid state's loss of hegemony was an instrumental formalism—a rationalized pragmatism of which the chosen instrument, naturally, was a new administrative structure and an important shift in the locus of decision-making power from old-line bureaucrats to a cadre largely composed of militarily trained technocrats.

The New Cabinet Structure

Botha announced his sweeping administrative reforms in 1979. Although it has taken until 1983 for the full intent of these changes to be realized, South Africa's method of operation and its ability to accomplish its business have been transformed by the shift from 20 to 4 cabinet committees, the primacy given formally and informally to the refurbished SSC, the concomitant expansion of the Office of the Prime Minister and the creation of a cabinet secretariat, the distribution of agendas and the keeping of minutes, the punctiliousness with which the paper flow is regulated, and the role that the military now plays in the entire process.

The Westminster model presumes the sovereignty of parliament, with a cabinet and a prime minister responsible to and acting on behalf of parliament. Nominally, South Africa's new arrangements adhered to such democratic principles, but their practice deviates markedly from them. As it has developed, the system as reshaped under Botha bypasses the cabinet and parliament to a degree that is new even for South Africa, Infogate included. The untidiness of the past has been replaced, certainly formally, by a new accountability and tightened organizational flows. But if this process serves South Africa well, it does so by elevating the goals of bureaucratic achievement and policy coordination above those of meaningful political participation and the development of a national consensus.

South Africa's cabinet now meets every Tuesday during the parliamentary session from mid-morning until well into the afternoon. There are agendas, and minutes are kept. Dr. J.P. Roux, who has the title of secretary-general of the newly renamed Office of the Prime Minister, organizes the cabinet's affairs and sees that its decisions are implemented. In his role, he is at the center of a carefully spun web that encompasses the committees, the permanent secretariat, and the interdepartmental committees (which also offer questions, and sometimes answers, to the cabinet committees). Roux is also charged with the task of prodding and coordinating the implementation of cabinet decisions by departments and parastatal bodies.

This analysis, and the time (longer than in Vorster's day) devoted to the deliberations of the cabinet, implies an accretion, not a diminution, of cabinet-level power. In one sense this is correct, for the prime minister has shifted certain kinds of decisions from his own (or from Vorster-like)

shoulders to the collectivity of the cabinet. He spends time in cabinet meetings constructing a consensus, something that no previous South African prime minister since Jan Christiaan Smuts ever sought to do. In 1982 and 1983, the cabinet met at great length to thrash out the details of the new constitutional legislation. Because there were major cleavages within the cabinet, with opposing points of view being represented by the most powerful members of that body, the proposals of the cabinet committees and their principals were subject to the kinds of cabinet-level review that nowadays are reserved for controversies and events that are extraordinary.

The serious issues on which there is substantive discussion are nevertheless few, and the most important do not under the present system necessarily come before the cabinet at all. Furthermore, because of the new committee system, and the seniority and influence of the ministers who chair the various committees, decisions made by the committees are by and large merely ratified by the cabinet, simply noted, or never discussed. (The future of Namibia is an example of a subject that is rarely discussed.) The less senior ministers say little, and certainly do not speak on matters outside their own portfolios. The amount of time devoted to cabinet meetings is therefore largely a reflection of the increasing complexity of government business, the emergence of far-reaching and time-consuming issues such as the new constitution, and (above all) a new emphasis on tactics, on the merchandising of policies, and on devising methods of handling the increasingly acrimonious and acid attacks on the government in parliament by parties of the right and left.

The Three Other Committees

Although the State Security Council has functioned in its new manner since September 1979, the three other committees of the cabinet have only in the last year begun to be fully operational. Whereas the SSC has a secretariat of 45, not counting its subordinate working committees, these other cabinet committees have small (five-man) secretariats, including some part-time members whose other work is performed directly for the Office of the Prime Minister.

The three committees are Financial and Economic Affairs, Social Affairs, and Constitutional Affairs. Minister of Finance Owen Horwood presides over the first; Minister of Cooperation and Development Pieter Koornhof runs the second; and Minister of Constitutional Development and Planning J. Christiaan Heunis has been in charge of the third.

Financial and Economic Affairs has a remarkable degree of autonomy, its decisions being regarded (probably erroneously) as largely technical and nonpolitical. Its secretariat is staffed by and draws upon the most financially and economically sophisticated talent in the Office of the Prime Minister, in the Reserve Bank, and in the Department of Finance.

The Social Affairs Committee has limited legitimacy, largely because Koornhof is perceived as having lost initiative and influence within the cabinet and within the ruling circles of the party. Many, if not all, of the issues that would be presumed to be "social" (i.e. those having an impact upon or altering the circumstances and welfare of Africans, Coloureds, and Asians) are dealt with almost exclusively in the Constitutional Committee, over which Heunis presides with a firm hand. Koornhof sits on that committee, as does the prime minister, Minister of Defense Malan, Minister of Police Louis le Grange, and Minister of Justice H.J. (Kobie) Coetsee. Major decisions concerning the tricameral parliament to be established when the new constitution comes into force, the President's Council, legislation to change the status of black urban dwellers, and influx control—in general, the shape and pace of reform—have been made by this committee.

These committees meet fortnightly throughout the parliamentary session and sporadically (unlike the SSC)

throughout the rest of the year. Their meeting dates are staggered so that ministers can regularly attend the meetings of more than a single committee. None of these activities conflicts with the convening every Monday of the SSC, and some meet before the cabinet convenes on Tuesdays. Since agendas are circulated beforehand, ministers other than those who are the official members of each of the committees are theoretically free to attend those meetings which interest or involve their own departments. Sometimes they do, but for the most part less senior ministers attend only those committees to which they are specifically invited.

Senior ministers are members of two or three committees (and sometimes also have seats on the SSC). The result is obvious: decisions of the cabinet are made by a subset of the total cabinet, either individually or together in the various cabinet committees, often with a full discussion only in the committees, if there. One caveat is that the prime minister cannot and does not attend all of the committee meetings. Important decisions are obviously discussed with him before they reach the committee stage, and monitored by one or more officials from his office. Decisions in all nonsecurity areas are probably also discussed beforehand with Heunis.

In addition to staff support supplied to each by a small secretariat, each of the three lesser cabinet committees is served by a subordinate working group convened and managed by the head of the committee secretariat and composed of high-level civil servants from the ministries concerned and, usually, a representative or two from the SSC. Nearly all of the decisions of the committees are prefigured by the working groups. The working groups raise issues, provide answers, and order the writing of the option papers that form the staple of the committee decision-making process. Ministers do give directions through the secretariats to these groups, but a crucial level of analysis and debate takes place intensely in these groups.

This intermediate process doubtless limits the ultimate

range of options presented to the ministerial committees. It is in the working groups that interdepartmental rivalries become apparent, and compromises are struck. Notable, too, is the presence on each of the working groups of representatives of the military and the police. In the formulation of legislation (the postponed Orderly Movement and Settlement of Persons Bill comes immediately to mind), security considerations (in the case of the aforementioned bill, the concern with combating urban terrorism) had an influence that was visible and pervasive. During the Vorster years, van den Bergh was personally regarded with suspicion by members of the cabinet, which limited his influence over legislation. But P.W. Botha has arranged his new decision-making machinery so that how individual items of legislation conform or do not conform to the concept of "total strategy" becomes a regular refrain. Overall the SSC and the other three committees are but a part of what Botha and the military have conceived of as a National Security Management System, for the defense of the Republic.

The State Security Council

At the heart of the management system, and central to all of P.W. Botha's plans for himself, his government, and his country, is the State Security Council. The prime minister chairs its meetings. He is joined by the statutory members: Malan, Coetsee, le Grange, and Minister of Foreign Affairs Roelof (Pik) Botha. In addition, Koornhof was invited to attend in 1979 and remains a member; so does Minister of Finance Owen Horwood. But the most influential minister after the prime minister is Heunis, who chairs the meetings if the prime minister is absent. Other regular members are the directors-general of Foreign Affairs and Justice, the head of the police, the chief of the Defense Force, the director of the National Intelligence Service (NIS), and Dr. Roux, a total of 14. From time to time other individuals are invited to address or meet with the SSC. The SSC takes its decisions by consensus, but the forming of a consensus usually follows the lead of the prime minister, Heunis, and Malan.

What is immediately apparent is the number of ministers who are not members of the SSC. Furthermore, the notion of cabinet responsibility and their own positions as ministers is devalued within the government by the presence in the innermost decision-making councils of the state of nonelected officials, three of whom are responsible for implementing "total strategy." The composition of the SSC, as much as the prime minister's command of it, narrows the government's legislative focus and also must preordain the kinds of subjects that are addressed, as well as the approach to each. Additionally, given its size, status, and direction, the concerns and the conclusions of the SSC must inevitably influence, inhibit, and overshadow the three other cabinet committees as well as the entire functioning of the Botha government.

Even if its subject matter and membership did not give the SSC a preeminent status in the government, it would still be able to achieve significant leverage by virtue of its size, organization, and bureaucratic resources. Lieutenant-General Andries Jacobus van Deventer, the secretary of the SSC, commands the "working committees" (which correspond to the "working groups" of the other cabinet committees) of the SSC, which itself is composed (as far as one can find out) primarily of officials from the military and police, Justice, and Foreign Affairs. But van Deventer also has a staff, which serves him, and which is nine times the size of the largest staffs servicing the other cabinet committees.

Van Deventer monitors everything that goes on at the cabinet and subcabinet level. He sits as a member of the working groups of the three other cabinet committees and shares with Brigadier John Huyser, a retired intelligence officer, the responsibility for vetting and channeling all policy papers destined for subcabinet or cabinet consideration. They perform this latter task as the directors of the permanent cabinet secretariat. Seventy percent of the membership of the secretariat is drawn from the military. Twenty percent comes from the NIS, and 10 percent from the Department of Foreign Affairs. Van Deventer's deputy is General G.J.F. van Rensburg.

Below the secretariat, and also subordinate to the working groups and the working committee, are 15 interdepartmental committees. Organizationally, they emanate from and report to the SSC, and are the originators of nearly all policy recommendations. The membership of the interdepartmental committees consists principally of heads of departments and of their senior deputies, legal advisors, and so on. A representative of the Defense Force sits on each committee and reports to van Deventer. Foreign Affairs is represented only on four of the interdepartmental committees; other ministries are represented on no more than and usually less than that number.

Van Deventer, now 53, was chief of staff of the finance division of the Defense Force before 1979. He worked closely with the prime minister when Botha was minister of defense under Vorster, and regards himself as the person chosen because of this long association to bring a military-style order to a hitherto uncoordinated government. Van Deventer thinks of himself as a careful planner, as a facilitator, as a good manager of paper flow on behalf of a prime minister who appreciates meticulous, precise management, good staffing, and appropriate follow-through. The prime minister insists on fully researched options before decisions can be contemplated. However, the extent to which "fully researched" means objective analysis cannot be ascertained. In any case, sloppy thinking is less often tolerated under the National Security Management System than it was before Botha came to power.

The military mind has thus clearly imposed itself on the workings of the South African government, but that mind appears to be primarily technocratic and functional and not (as yet) given to Latin American-type designs on the transformation or capture of the state. Those kinds of prescriptive possibilities have doubtless occurred to some officers now serving at the heart of the bureaucratic endeavor, particularly if they have viewed inefficiency and (perish the thought) chicanery in the ranks of civilian government. But the managerial revolution is still a servant of a more cautious, politically led reorientation of South Africa's style of governance.

The SSC effectively makes decisions and influences many that are not directly its own. As its name implies, all security (military and police) questions are brought to it, and it follows from the South African doctrine of total onslaught and total strategy that almost every aspect of modern government in South Africa can be construed to have security implications. Moreover, and much more basic to an understanding of who runs South Africa today, and how it may continue to run, the SSC has become the court of virtually final resort for a broad range of national issues.

The future of Namibia, for example, is hardly a matter of solely parochial concern. It is linked to a bundle of domestic and external political issues, questions involving intricate negotiations with the West and with Angola, tactics for counterrevolutionary actions within the territory and across its borders, economic and financial concerns, social matters, and so on. How South Africa resolves the problem of Namibia will have a direct impact on the entire future security, economic well-being, and political survival of white South Africa itself. Yet, if the fate of Namibia were ever an issue discussed by the representatives of the (white) electorate of South Africa, that day is past. Strategy and tactics on Namibia are decided upon in the SSC whenever those decisions have not already been preempted by a military action of some kind. Did the military decide to undo Dirk Mudge, leader of the Democratic Turnhalle Alliance, before or after a decision was taken in the SSC? Was the decision to back Peter Kalangula of the National Democratic Party made in Namibia by the military command, or by the SSC? The SSC probably has authorized the overall direction of preemptive strikes into Angola, leaving the chain of military command to work out the precise details. It regulates the flow of supplies to Jonas Savimbi's UNITA. It has sanctioned the cease-fire talks with Angola. It decides how and when to respond to Western initiatives. Moreover, each decision of this kind began, whether implicitly or actually, as an option to be presented to the SSC. The positions on which the options were based started as military, or sometimes foreign affairs, initiatives.

The range of possibilities presented to the SSC need not emerge from the deliberations of the working committee in especially broad forms. The influence of the "doves," including the foreign minister and his director-general, is limited by the preponderance of "hawks" at all levels of this new decision-making apparatus. Observers are certain, for example, that Pik Botha and his department have relatively little influence in today's decision-making arena; from a structural viewpoint, personalities aside, it is understandable why he and his department should feel so powerless beside the juggernaut of the technocratic, military machine.

If the Department of Foreign Affairs has relatively little clout within the SSC, obviously those departments which are not represented on the SSC, and are not consulted (even in the cabinet), can have less impact on decisions. Minister of National Education Gerrit Viljoen, who had previously served as the administrator-general of Namibia, presumably is a Namibian expert. But he is not on the SSC and formally seldom learns about or is asked to advise on the day-to-day running of the territory he once administered by fiat. Foreign Affairs no longer has a direct say about Namibia's internal governance either. The new administrator-general and his principal civilian deputy report to the Office of the Prime Minister, while the commanding general in Namibia has his military chain of command which eventually leads to the SSC.

Whether to raid Maseru, support the MNR in Mozambique, give aid to Zimbabwean dissidents, and try to purchase long-range reconnaissance aircraft are obviously decisions within the ultimate purview of the SSC. In the case of the December 1982 raid into the Lesotho capital of Maseru, for example, the Defense Force seems to have had prior approval in principle from the SSC, but the cabinet was not informed beforehand. Moreover, the Defense Force appears to have chosen the precise date and method in accord with general rather than specific instructions.

The SSC involves itself in a much broader range of decisions, too. It is interested in land transfers such as the 1982 attempt to cede the KaNgwane part of KwaZulu and part of Ingwavumaland to Swaziland. It has a say about the overall policy regarding trade unions, detentions without trial, the shape of the new Defense Force legislation (including the issue of conscientious objection), the character of social legislation (particularly that giving further prerogatives to Africans), and the broadening of educational opportunities. In the case of the Orderly Movement and Settlement of Persons bill, representatives of the military staff of the SSC joined forces with the civil servants from Koornhof's own department to defeat his reform endeavors in the constitutional committee. The bill that emerged was not one that Koornhof wanted, but security considerations had prevailed. They may yet do so with regard to other aspects of Koornhof's urban reform program.

Who Governs?

The formal mechanism of decision making in South Africa gives the SSC a primary role and the three other cabinet committees important, but (except for the Finance and Economic Committee) lesser ones. Because the SSC and the other committees are subject to direct and indirect influence by well-entrenched civil servants, and since so many of those civil servants are in fact seconded military officers, it is evident that the real levers of formal power in South Africa are no longer controlled exclusively, or as much as they were, or even as much as the South African public may think they are, by elected representatives of the (white) people. Indeed, the National Security Management System has superseded the cabinet, the party, and the electorate in many areas. A saving grace, if that is the word, is that the prime minister is in ultimate control, assisted by at least one other elected party member and the chain of military command. Furthermore, complete military dominance of the decision-making machinery is tempered by the nonmilitary bureaucrats' awareness of their weakened position, a suspicion of military designs, and the natural infighting that occurs when one institution has been invaded by another.

Even as the authority of the cabinet has become increasingly titular, the National Party has also undergone a dramatic loss of power. There still are parliamentary study committees on virtually all subjects, but the power of their chairmen (backbench members of the National Party) to hold ministers to account has diminished. Where the caucus retains much of its power is not on particular decisions but on the very broad reach of national policy. The prime minister must still take heed of the risk of revolt among his backbenchers on issues such as the constitutional reform. But he can ignore them on Namibia, on "destabilization," on trade unions, and so on. And while neither Botha nor the military bureaucrats can ignore the backbenchers on issues of constituency concern, such as borehole drilling and perimeter defense, those are more matters of politics than decision making.

Beyond the party caucus are the provincial congresses — historically the inner core and the strength of the National Party. The prime minister used the provincial machinery skillfully in 1982 when he sought the congresses' necessary consent for the updated version of his constitutional plan, but he does not seek their advice on security matters or Namibia. There are also provincial legislatures and officials, but their influence on national or party policy has been diminished under Botha.

The role in the decision-making process of commissions of inquiry, composed of experts, of presumed adjudicators (e.g., judges), or of a cross section of the power elite, has varied. Since the formation of commissions is used throughout the world to defer or permanently postpone decisions, it comes as no surprise that official South Africa has found it expedient from time to time to give intractable problems to supposedly impartial commissions in the hope that the very calling of a commission will make the problem go away or that the passage of time will make recommendations electorally or internationally palatable. Some commissions have studied a problem and, from the government's view, exceeded their mandate by proposing solutions too radical for the prime minister, the party, the civil service, or all three. Other commissions, mostly those attempting to solve problems in areas where the government knows it must advance, but cannot think how, have, because of a sufficiently broad and influential membership, a decisive and well-connected chairman, or both, altered the perceptions of the government itself.

Some of the academically led commissions can be expected to develop their own sources of information and analysis. Normally that function is performed by a seconded bureaucracy. Insofar as those seconded staffs will now be drawn, even partially, from the SSC and the military, an additional lever will be added to the influence of the Defense Force on South African decision making.

Do the departments (ministries) themselves still matter? Clearly, no matter how well the SSC and the other committees coordinate, prod, and push, the machinery of implementation remains in the departments. The departments have admittedly lost a share of the available overall finances, which, in any institutional power struggle, go to the favored and the swift, especially if the favored and the swift are guiding the ship of state. The SSC, through its mostly military representatives, can learn what is happening and why, and can certainly poke and extoll the departments through the interdepartmental committees — but the drafting of legislation is still done in departments. South African bureaucrats are especially adept at dragging their

feet and working to rule; they know and make the regulations, too. Thus, the cooperation of the departments is necessary before decisions can be implemented.

What has been described thus far is the formal process
used in South Africa to arrive at decisions. The process is
intended to be methodical and systematic, and intolerant of
shortcuts. Intentionally painstaking, it can only be implemented by an enlarged coordinating bureaucracy. And it
takes time, especially if policy directives and actual legislation are to reflect new kinds and degrees of staff attention.

This is a system which could prepare for crises and
emergencies, but could only rarely cope with them in an
instantaneous fashion. It may be a system more efficient
than the informal one employed in Vorster's day, but it is
cumbersome. Therefore, a description and analysis of the
formal decision-making capacity and machinery of the
South African state can only partially answer the crucial
question: Is the new machinery actually employed when
those who rule South Africa make the decisions that count?

Vorster and van den Bergh made the important decisions in their time. Vorster also had golfing friends and
corporate cronies. Representatives of some kinds of institutions used contacts to reach Vorster himself, to obtain either favorable decisions or other forms of help at one or
more levels of government. From impressionistic evidence,
it appears that Vorster gathered most of his ideas, information, and insights from his tight-knit circles of friends.
Most of those friends were from the private sector, and
Vorster was never loath to bypass official channels (the
Muldergate scandal makes this point perfectly evident).
Vorster's staff work was rudimentary and his colleagues
and his party caucus rarely knew precisely how or why key
decisions were made.

Today this process is supposed to be different. But is
it? Botha has a new set of friends and is not known for his
golf. But he is close to Malan and other military officers. He
relies on the advice of Heunis and Vice President Alwyn
Schlebusch. He frequently talks to industrialists.

In crises, Malan and Heunis rush to Botha's side as van den Bergh went to Vorster's. Ad hoc decisions are still made on or recorded on the backs of envelopes. Someone in high places, for example, decided to back the 1981 attempt to overthrow the government of the Seychelles. The SSC, it is understood, did not know about it, although sections of the military and the NIS were aware of the preparations that were revealed in court. The now-aborted Swaziland land swap seems to have been initiated in the upper reaches of the Department of Foreign Affairs and never to have been subjected to full SSC or cabinet scrutiny. Responses to key American or Angolan diplomatic communications are probably required too urgently to be left to percolate through each of the levels of the SSC. If a swift response were needed in the wake of, say, the death of a neighboring monarch or the ouster of a neighboring head of state, it would be equally difficult to formulate policy through the SSC. Overall, South Africa still lacks what U.S. Assistant Secretary for African Affairs Chester Crocker once described (in *South Africa's Defense Posture: Coping with Vulnerability*, CSIS/SAGE Washington Paper No. 84, 1981) as a capacity for sophisticated threat assessment and political analysis.

No modern executive is fully accountable. No matter how punctilious the procedures and ironclad the rules have become, it is hardly plausible that Botha acts only when he has proper briefing books and full analyses. A volatile person, he naturally responds to decisive moments, even if to do so may mean bending his own strictures about the need for "research." Moreover, decisions made by ad hoc methods by Botha, or by Malan, by the chief of the Defense Force (e.g., the Maseru raid), or even by Major-General Charles Lloyd in Namibia/Angola, are ones more important and more injurious than those which usually filter up through the SSC and the other committees.

In noting the distinction between formal and informal modes of decision making and the different kinds of decisions that are made in both spheres, it should also be apparent that the membrane between formal and informal is permeable. The informal impinges upon and influences the formal. The formal validates and covers up for the informal. Prime ministers are known to come to cabinet (and now SSC) meetings with their own plans, or plans devised after talking to all manner of outsiders from different parts of the private sector.

Decisions that are unfortunate for South Africa, defined in this context merely as those (e.g., the death of Steve Biko) which generate unfavorable publicity, need not have been made through the formal channels. If a preemptive strike on a neighboring nation infuriates the West, that is one kind of decision where an agreement in principle, made initially at high levels (if not through the stated channels), may become a counterproductive act if the scale, the timing, or the side effects of the strike conform insufficiently to the original policy directive. And the military leadership may have an agenda different (as it does in Namibia) from those of most, if not all, civilian politicians. The entire regional destabilization policy may fit under this rubric.

But where South Africa suffers most (even under the National Security Management System) is when middle-level officials react traditionally or exceed instructions. Or, possibly, they obey the letter of outdated or ill-conceived instructions from their superiors. The death of Saul Mkhize, defending his land in the southeastern Transvaal, is an example of a general decision (to continue removals), followed by a high-level decision (one presumes) to move against the particular Driefontein Black Spot and to ignore African protests, followed by the maladroit implementation of orders by low-ranking bureaucrats. It is unlikely that any management system, no matter how efficient, can rapidly alter the reflexes of rank-and-file officials. Moreover, given the structure of South Africa, it is probably unreasonable to expect the National Security Management System to think through the consequences at the implementation level of all varieties of decisions that flow from a policy framework (in this case apartheid) with so many givens, precedents, and shibboleths. Botha does not intend his new military-manned system to transform South Africa. He merely wants the tactical (not the strategic) posture of his administration to be coherent and coordinated.

Individuals influence decision makers informally. So do institutions. Botha's government is much less influenced by or intertwined with the Broederbond than was Vorster's. The Dutch Reformed Church has declined in its immediate influence on the leaders of the present government, and also nationally. The Afrikaans-speaking business community has access to Botha and his government. The police have a say. The Departments of Foreign Affairs and of Cooperation and Development have less influence than before. The old-line bureaucracy battles against change, and does manage to slow Botha's pursuit of reform. But, aside from the party and the cabinet, it is obviously the military which is the leading decision-making institution in today's South Africa, both because of Botha's belief in its abilities and its clear-sightedness and because he ascended to the top without a range of other powerful national connections.

South Africa is still a long way, however, from becoming a jackboot state in the Latin American sense. Among important countervailing tendencies that will tend to block any conversion to Prussian-style government is the inertia of a bloated bureaucracy (including the parastatals). Yet, Botha shares the military's vision of a fortress South Africa, tactically reformed, but strategically sound if not hegemonic. The soldiers are his chosen instrument and he is theirs.

The New Constitution

The formal system, as described, is eminently adaptable to the strong executive presidency to be established under the new constitution approved by the white voters on November 2, 1983. What works in a nominal parliamentary democracy will work even more efficiently within the overall framework of the new constitution. Indeed, one supposes that the SSC would become even more central to the functioning of the new arrangement, serving (as in a sense it now does) as the secretariat of the presidential system. If so, the other three committees of the cabinet may become less important, even as the cabinet, the parliament (now to be tricameral), and the party caucus lose whatever residual powers each still retains. One can foresee a greater centralization of power under the new system. The military will run the SSC, involve itself more and more in affairs of state, and certainly not lessen its institutional influence on the future shape of South Africa.

3

A Guide to Black Politics in South Africa

Steven McDonald

November 1984

Under the terms of the new constitution approved by the white electorate in November 1983, South Africa's whites-only legislature was replaced on September 3, 1984 by a parliament consisting of the incumbent 178-member House of Assembly representing South Africa's 4.5 million whites, a newly-elected 85-member House of Representatives for the country's 2.7 million Coloureds (mixed race), and a newly elected 45-member House of Deputies for the Indian (i.e. Asian) population of some 870,000. The constitution makes no provision for parliamentary representation of the country's 22 million blacks. P.W. Botha, who was sworn in as the Republic's executive president on September 14, after receiving a unanimous vote from an electoral college appointed by the new tricameral parliament, has gained a number of powers beyond those he held as prime minister. These include the right to decide (immune from challenge in the courts) what matters are and are not the "own affair" of any of the three ethnic houses of parliament or a shared "general affair" of the nation. President Botha also has the authority to veto any legislation passed by any house of parliament.

Ironically, the new constitution has caused rifts within and between the white, Coloured, and Indian communities while having an opposite effect on the black majority it ignores. Although an unexpectedly high proportion (66 percent) of white voters approved the arrangement in the 1983 referendum, the Coloured and Indian electorates were less enthusiastic. In parliamentary elections held in late August in those two communities, the official turnouts were just over 20 percent and about 30 percent respectively of registered voters. Moreover, the voting was accompanied by protest demonstrations and school boycotts (at one point 630,000 Coloured students were out of classes). Government officials have blamed intimidation as well as a lack of organization and of "democratic traditions" for the low voter turnout.

Black South Africans, on the other hand, have rallied against the constitution, forging an unparalleled degree of unity on this issue and achieving some notable success in protest politics as they urged their Coloured and Indian compatriots to stay away from the polls. Of course, the durability of this new communality is debatable for a number of reasons—notably, its focus on a single issue, the formidable coercive powers of the South African government, and the government's demonstrated willingness to use these powers (see Section 9 below). Meanwhile, the new restrictions imposed on the freedom of action of externally based forces of black South African nationalism by the Nkomati Accord and other regional "nonaggression" pacts have also created new pressures and challenges for internal black activists across the political spectrum.

The following is a summary assessment of the organizational structure of black power in South Africa as of the latter half of 1984:

1. The African National Congress (ANC)

The ANC is the oldest nationalist organization in sub-Saharan Africa. Its roots go back to early pan-Africanist and nationalist thinkers of the late nineteenth century, many of whom were educated in the United States. Organizational-ly, it developed from the South African Native Convention, which met in 1909 to protest the terms of the draft consti-tution for South African union following the Boer War. The Convention's protests were ineffective and, in frustration, the South African Native National Congress – subsequent-ly renamed the African National Congress – was formed in 1912.

The ANC's early philosophy was moderate, indeed al-most archaic, compared with its present profile. It was founded by professional, middle-class Africans who focused on, according to its 1919 constitution, the use of "resolu-tions, protests . . . constitutional and peaceful propaganda . . . deputations [and] enquiries" to reach its objectives. Those objectives were clearly evolutionary, ranging from demands for "equitable justice" in the 1909 Convention to the All-African Convention's call in the 1930s for "reconsideration" of unjust laws and protests of the removal of Africans from the voters' rolls in Cape Province. The ANC of that era was willing to accept a qualified franchise for blacks based on "civilized" factors such as education, property, or wage qual-ifications, and it expressed its understanding of and con-cern for the protection of white interests.

Over the years, the ANC inexorably moved toward a greater radicalism, from early petition to protest to defi-ance, then to underground insurgency, banning, and exile. This escalation was due to growing frustration over a lack of any results from peaceful and legal protests (e.g., the failure to block the removal of Cape Africans from the vot-ers' rolls in 1936). The ANC was also stimulated by the post-World War II idealism (in particular the self-determi-nation principles of the Atlantic Charter) and stymied by the coming to power of the Afrikaner-based National Party in 1948 and the implementation of apartheid that followed.

The ANC's 1952 "Defiance Campaign" was the first mass civil disobedience campaign in South Africa. Another effort to broaden the ANC's base was the Congress Alli-ance, which brought together Indian, Coloured, and white

organizations in protest against growing government repression. Certain individual African members of the South
African Communist Party (SACP) had participated in the
ANC since the 1920s, but played no formative role in its
organization. After the SACP was banned in 1950, more
white and Indian Communists began to involve themselves
through the broadening Congress Alliance. The Defiance
Campaign itself was an outcome of a decision, initiated
largely by the newly formed Youth League, to begin a program of mass action. The Freedom Charter, issued by the
Alliance in 1955, resulted in growing harassment, bannings,
and detentions by the government. Thousands of arrests
took place as antipassbook marches, protests, and boycotts
increased in number. The long-running Treason Trial of
1956–1961, in which 156 persons were charged but ultimately acquitted, was a central event in this era of border-
line legality for the ANC.

Following the Sharpeville confrontation in 1960, in
which police fired on a nonviolent demonstration, killing 67
Africans and wounding 186, the ANC was banned and went
underground. In 1961, its leadership, along with some
white and Indian Communists, formed a paramilitary sabotage unit called Umkhonto we Sizwe ("Spear of the Nation").
In 1962 and 1963, the Umkhonto leadership, including
Nelson Mandela, was arrested. By the end of 1964 the bulk
of ANC leadership was either in detention or in exile.

For the past 20 years, the ANC has directed its activities from headquarters in Lusaka (Zambia) and has also
maintained offices in London, New York, and several other
countries. The first decade of its exile was relatively quiescent. By the mid-1970s, however, a low-key insurgency campaign had been launched, consisting mainly of sabotage
and attacks on government installations that resulted in
only a few fatalities. In the 1980s, the campaign has been
stepped up, becoming more sophisticated and exacting a
higher death toll.

The sabotage action against the Koeberg nuclear power
station in December 1982 and at the Sasol coal conver-

sion plant in June 1980; attacks on police stations and government offices; and the May 1983 car bombing outside air force offices in Pretoria (at least 18 deaths and 217 injuries) added up to a clear new trend. Guerrilla activities have occurred in all of South Africa's four provinces and in most major urban centers, including Johannesburg, Durban, Bloemfontein, Cape Town, and Pretoria. By these diverse actions, the ANC has sought to demonstrate an ability to strike anywhere and to penetrate sophisticated defenses of critical installations. A rash of bombings throughout the country, concentrated around the month of the Coloured and Indian elections, as well as a major attack on the Mobil refinery in Durban in May 1984, have been intended to send a message. This message is that the "nonaggression" pacts South Africa has signed with Mozambique and Swaziland, and seeks with others, all involving denial of "bases" to the ANC, will not end the movement's effectiveness.

The ANC has always been identified by its adherence to nonracialism in its campaign for political rights in South Africa. The Freedom Charter, which enshrines its basic philosophy, advocates a "South Africa which belongs to all who live in it, black and white." The leadership has publicly spoken against racial confrontation and consistently calls for a "new nonracial democratic South Africa." An irony of this nonracism is that the presence of whites within the ANC command structure, seen by some as an indication of the organization's broad appeal, feeds the South African government's belief that the movement is dominated by the South African Communist Party and by the Soviet Union.

Individual Communists within the party hierarchy have considerable influence and played a role in moving the ANC from peaceful protest to greater activism. Since its exile, the movement has received the bulk of its weaponry and much of its training from the Soviet Union and other Eastern bloc nations, a familiar pattern in African and Third World nations confronting minority or colonial ruling groups.

In sum, the ANC receives more international recognition and media attention than any other black South African organization. The ANC's ability to shape and influence events inside South Africa beyond the pressures exerted through its sabotage campaign, however, will be dependent on internal black perceptions of its various parts, the character of other emerging internal organizations, and the coercive and co-optive powers of the South African government.

2. The Pan-Africanist Congress (PAC)

The PAC was formed in 1959 by a group of ANC members who were uncomfortable with the vague socialism and multiracial approach of the ANC. The thrust behind the PAC's formation derived in part from black suspicions of Indian and white Communist activists and their external connections, but the underlying theme of the new movement was a purified form of African nationalism. The founders viewed the ANC Freedom Charter as a betrayal of that principle. While rejecting white alliances, the PAC was also strongly anti-Communist. Many members of the ANC Youth League, which had also been urging a more nationalist line, moved into the PAC over time.

The PAC's founder-leader was Robert Sobukwe – imprisoned in 1960, later released but banned in Kimberley. An intellectual who practiced law after his release, Sobukwe strongly influenced the founders of the Black Consciousness movement (see below). When he died of cancer in 1978, the funeral in his home at Graaff-Reinet was attended by hundreds of Black Consciousness adherents as well as old-line nationalists of the PAC and ANC.

After their post-Sharpeville banning, the PAC and the ANC formed an alliance called the South African United Front. This quickly fell apart, however, due to various ideological and personal conflicts. Since then, the PAC, unlike the ANC, has not been able to organize effectively outside South Africa. It has an external structure, with offices in

New York, London, Dar es Salaam, and other African capitals, but, especially since Sobukwe's death, has had a weak leadership marked by dissension, including assassination. The PAC has nonetheless maintained considerable support within South Africa and occasionally launches guerrilla operations, although not on a scale comparable with those of the ANC. The movement has undergone something of a resurgence recently in the general rise of black activism against the new constitution.

3. The Azanian People's Organization (AZAPO)

AZAPO is the political home of the Black Consciousness movement and the heir to the organizations that were banned by the government in 1977. Black Consciousness is more a philosophy than an ideology and, while it has always had organizational ramifications, it was never an organization as such. It grew intellectually from the same roots as Pan-Africanism, Negritude, Black Pride, and Black Power. Its development followed a Black Theology group in South Africa strongly influenced by Americans such as Jim Cones and Martin Luther King, Jr.

Black Consciousness began to emerge as an identifiable philosophy in the late 1960s, reaching its peak of public recognition and organizational adherence in the early to mid-1970s. Over time, Steve Biko became its best-known spokesman, although he was only one of many who helped to form and continued to develop the philosophy. Barney Pityana, Ben Khoapa, Mokethi Mothlabi, Mamphela Ramphele, Thoko Mbanjwa, Drake Koka, Saths Cooper, Malusi Mpumlawana, and many others played important roles in the movement.

Organizationally, Black Consciousness surfaced first in such student groupings as the South African Students' Organization (SASO) and the South African Students' Movement (SASM) — partly in reaction to white students' groups' efforts to broaden their representation among black students. The political arm, the Black People's Convention (BPC), was formed in 1972 to provide "a political home for all Black people who could not reconcile themselves to working within the framework of separate development, and to promote Black solidarity." One of the principles of Black Consciousness was self-help, and, accordingly, organizations such as the Black Community Programmes, the Ginzberg Education Fund, the Zenophile Clinic, and other community, health, educational, and agricultural schemes were established.

Black Consciousness is generally perceived today, by both its detractors and proponents, as a radical, racially exclusive philosophy. Its roots lie with the PAC rather than the ANC. Current adherents eschew alliances with multiracial groups. Black Consciousness's original philosophy seemed to suggest a less exclusivist policy, focusing on black pride and development and promoting a liberation sequence, i.e. independence of person, then community, then nation. Although it was revolutionary in the sense that it challenged the existing social, economic, and political orders, it was not intended as a denial of a role for whites. Biko saw few whites as potential allies, but he also took the position that "Blacks have had enough experience as the objects of racism not to wish to reverse the tables." Black Consciousness, he said, was "the affirmation of black humans that emancipates black people from white racism and thus provides an authentic freedom for both . . . it affirms the humanity of white people in that it says *no* to white oppression."

Almost all of the early Black Consciousness organizations were banned in 1977, along with most of the movement's important leaders. Black Consciousness was once more represented by a political organization, however, with the formation of AZAPO in 1978. Created in Soweto by former members of the Soweto Student Representative Council and of the BPC, AZAPO had a low profile during its first years, except for the national attention it received when it worked with Father Patrick Matelengwe and family

members in planning the arrangements for Robert Sobukwe's funeral in 1978. There were strong Black Consciousness overtones in the funeral proceedings, and an incident having to do with an effort by Chief Mangosuthu G.
Buthelezi to speak almost resulted in serious harm to the
Zulu leader of Inkatha (see Inkatha, Section 4). Although
AZAPO had none of the known Black Consciousness leaders of the SASO/SASM/BPC period within its executive, it
became the standard bearer for the philosophy of these
groups and has developed a new cadre of leaders as well as
bringing old Black Consciousness types back with the formation of the National Forum (see Section 6).

4. InKatha yeNkululenko yeSizwe (Inkatha)

Inkatha is a Zulu cultural organization founded in 1928. Its
name means a woven grass ring used by peasant women to
cushion loads carried on their heads; figuratively, it denotes
the cushion between the people and their burdens. The
movement remained obscure for nearly half a century until
Chief Buthelezi revived it in 1974 to sidestep legal repression of political activity. The constitution adopted in 1975
describes Inkatha as a "national cultural movement" that
"desires to abolish all forms of discrimination and separation." In more political terms, Inkatha aims to span tribal
and urban-rural divisions and to bring change in an "orderly
and controllable fashion which will lead to a liberated South
Africa which is governable." Although Buthelezi is the chief
minister of KwaZulu, the government-designated Zulu
homeland, he and Inkatha reject homeland independence
and stand for a central, unified South Africa. Inkatha op-
poses the new constitution and calls for "a national convention" of blacks and whites to discuss the country's future.

Inkatha currently claims over 750,000 dues-paying
members, making it the largest black organization in South
Africa's history. It is very well organized, with a military-
style hierarchy and discipline. It has a central committee,

chaired by the movement's president (Buthelezi), and regional branches, including township outlets throughout the Transvaal. In KwaZulu (a 12,000-square-mile cluster of land parcels in Natal province), Inkatha has branches operating in most communities, including youth groups in schools and a Women's Brigade. The urban branches are not as tightly controlled, although meetings in Soweto, outside Johannesburg in the Transvaal, are well attended.

Inkatha says it is open to all black people and claims a large multiethnic following throughout the country. Secretary-General Oscar Dhlomo stated in an interview published in the quarterly *Leadership SA* (Vol. 3, no. 1, 1984) that 40 percent of Inkatha was non-Zulu as early as 1978 and cited an opinion poll result to support that claim. In the same interview, on the other hand, Dhlomo observed that the Zulus are the largest ethnic group in South Africa, that Zulu-dominated Natal is Inkatha's base, and that the organization is thus predominantly Zulu. On balance, despite its aspirations, Inkatha remains essentially a Zulu entity.

Criticism of Inkatha is varied and emotional. Many observers see it as a personal vehicle for the political aspirations of Buthelezi and claim that it would cease to exist without his presence. It is also criticized for using strongarm recruiting tactics in KwaZulu. Many fear its militaristic image, strengthened by Buthelezi's threats against his opponents. The killing of five students at the University of Zululand in October 1983 by Inkatha "impis" during campus protests and clashes added credibility to the concerns of Inkatha's critics.

Buthelezi has a thin skin and does not take criticism in stride, thus making Inkatha's attempts to seek a broader constituency and tactical alliances more difficult. Nevertheless, Inkatha stresses black unity and Buthelezi is personally sensitive to that need. In 1976, he formed a group called the Black Unity Front, consisting of the leaders of other homelands that had rejected independence and of the (Coloured) Labour Party. The Black Unity Front was expanded in subsequent years to include the (Indian) Reform Party and was renamed the South African Black Alliance. Under its new rubric, this attempt at unification foundered when the Labour Party opted to participate in the elections under the 1984 constitution. Inkatha has now established an alliance (the South African Federal Union) with black business, church, and homeland leaders brought together by their shared opposition to the new constitution (see Section 7).

Inkatha's relations with the ANC were quite cordial until 1979. Differences in the past five years have centered on Inkatha's rejection of violence and Buthelezi's position of opposition to foreign divestment or disinvestment from South Africa as well as other sanctions. During the early 1980s, personal animosities further weakened the ANC/Inkatha relationship. There was some early contact between Inkatha and the United Democratic Front (see Section 5); since the University of Zululand incident and Buthelezi's unwillingness to criticize or investigate it, however, links have been broken and the two groups are openly hostile to each other.

Yet Buthelezi remains a charismatic and dynamic leader, heading a large and powerful organization, which, as he likes to emphasize, is self-supporting financially. Because Inkatha is indisputably well organized, it has an enormous potential for contesting local elections or promoting strikes, boycotts, or work stayaways. Buthelezi is also an eloquent spokesman for black South Africa. Even Steve Biko, who strongly criticized Buthelezi's motivations and tactics, once said to me: "After all, Buthelezi is black. He knows and lives the problem and can tell the story."

5. The United Democratic Front (UDF)

The UDF is the broadest-based of the new political movements. Ideologically, it bears comparison with the ANC; organizationally, it resembles the Congress Alliance of the

1950s. Its birthdate is the year 1983, but its ideological roots are much older.

The UDF has attracted disparate groupings that have ties to the ANC but are uncomfortable with the ANC's exile status or its open advocacy of violence. The UDF has also acquired adherents from among blacks uncomfortable with the postbanning radicalization of the Black Consciousness movement and with the fact that no internal organization spoke for those who eschewed the exclusivist racial approach but still considered themselves "progressive" and antiapartheid. (In 1979, for example, at a conference held by AZAPO, a student wing was formed called the Azanian Students' Organization [AZASO]. Black Consciousness was, of course, the central theme for its formation, but subsequent attempts to form campus branches ran into difficulties and AZASO began to diverge ideologically from its parent. AZASO's then-president, Joe Phaahla, stated that "a number of students were not prepared to affiliate with a dogmatic approach," and, in 1981, AZASO broke with AZAPO, stating in its new charter that it embraced a broader, nonracial, more progressive outlook. By 1982, AZASO was seeking "to forge links with all relevant organizations concerned with the liberation of the oppressed and exploited people of South Africa [but] to continue to spread the nonracial gospel." AZASO later played a role in the formation of the UDF.)

The UDF seems to have begun to coalesce at a Johannesburg meeting in May 1983, at which 30 organizations representing trade union, civic, and church groups, along with AZASO, came together. The moving forces behind the Johannesburg meeting were the Transvaal Indian Congress, the Transvaal Anti-President's Council Committee, and the Anti-Community Council Committee. This meeting was, in part, inspired by a February 1983 speech by Dutch Reformed Church (Coloured) leader Dr. Alan Boesak, also currently the president of the World Alliance of Reformed Churches. Dr. Boesak had invited various organizations, including sports and civic bodies, to come together for "the struggle for a nonracial, open, democratic South Africa, a unitary state in which all the people will have the rights accorded them by God."

Although the UDF began to take shape in the Transvaal, its appeal rapidly became nationwide. Former ANC supporters and whites, Coloureds, and Indians, as well as Africans not comfortable with the tight ideological parameters of Black Consciousness, rallied to its banner. It was officially launched as a national movement at a convention in August 1983. Some 7,000 to 12,000 persons (estimates vary) representing over 400 diverse organizations met in Cape Town's Coloured township of Mitchell's Plain and pledged to fight "side by side against the government's constitutional proposals and the Koornhof bills." The latter were a set of parliamentary proposals relating to the pass laws, black residential rights, and township municipal powers. The UDF demanded a "true democracy [for] all South Africans" and "a single, nonracial, unfragmented South Africa . . . free of Bantustans and Group Areas."

The front's declared founders and patrons read like a "who's who" of black and white activists over the years, with a strong ANC flavor. They included Nelson Mandela, Walter Sisulu, Helen Joseph, Govan Mbeki, and Dennis Goldburg as patrons and Archie Gumede, Albertina Sisulu, and Oscar Mpetha as presidents.

Focused on the specific objective of opposing the new constitutional proposals, the UDF outlined a strategy of organizing, mobilizing, and educating to create unity among its followers and "to represent their views and aspirations." Organizationally, the UDF has a National General Council, but is decentralized into at least five regional bodies. It is essentially an umbrella organization. Individuals do not join directly but only through an organizational entity. Membership is claimed to be as much as 1 million people affiliated to 560 organizations.

The UDF actively lobbied among whites against the "yes" vote prior to the November 1983 referendum on the constitution; successfully campaigned against black participation in the December 1983 municipal council elections, holding the turnout down to some 10 percent in several townships countrywide; has regularly held rallies and distributed literature on such occasions as the anniversaries of the Sharpeville shootings and the Soweto-sparked upheavals of 1976; has spoken out on issues such as the Strydom Committee's recommendations on the Group Areas Act and on relocations; effectively mobilized (the government says through intimidation) opposition to the participation by Coloureds and Indians in the August parliamentary elections; and, during the election and postelection unrest in several black townships, organized medical, legal, and nutritional assistance for victims.

The UDF has also appealed to the international community for recognition and publicity. Dr. Boesak frequently travels abroad and speaks often about the UDF. In April 1984, the UDF Transvaal general secretary, Mohamed Valli, went to the United States, Canada, and Europe, and visited the United Nations, in search of "moral [and] political support [to] strengthen our hand internally."

Much of the UDF's rhetoric comes from the ANC Freedom Charter, which, ironically, the South African government has recently allowed to be distributed in the country. Although the UDF openly claims connection with many ANC members and includes in its ranks the Release Mandela Campaign group, statements made for public consumption by UDF officials disclaim any ANC organizational ties. There are differences with the ANC on a number of points—most notably over the use of violence—and some supporters, as noted above, may have come to the UDF out of frustration with the ANC. National Publicity Secretary Patrick Lekota, a former Black Consciousness activist, and other UDF supporters such as Winnie Mandela emphasize that the UDF is not meant as a substitute or rival for "accredited liberation movements" and that it is merely an "alliance of first-level organizations." Certainly many of its affiliates and supporters who are white or who have Black Consciousness roots would not welcome overt connections with the ANC.

Whether the reluctance to admit past or present ANC linkages is due to the factors cited publicly or merely an elaborate facade to avoid legal crackdowns arising from the ANC's banned status is difficult to determine. In any case, the UDF seems to be acquiring a life of its own. Even taking into account Lekota's emphasis on the umbrella nature of the organization, the sheer numbers and the focus on clear-cut tactical objectives warrant attention. The UDF now has a national, salaried executive, publishes literature, and has an efficient, democratic national structure that allows its members to vet policy issues thoroughly and recommend action. It works through affiliate members or empathetic white liberal organizations in establishing grass-roots community contact points.

The UDF is currently considering its strategies for what one official recently called the "ongoing struggle against the new system after its formal inauguration." Recent interviews with UDF leaders indicated that these "strategies" were not yet decided upon and probably would be defined by the membership. Still, the UDF's future is uncertain, largely because of possible government pressures (see Section 9) and because of the unattainability of its objectives in the foreseeable future, which creates built-in obsolescence or self-destructive tendencies.

6. The National Forum (NF)

The second and smaller black group formed to fight the new constitution is the National Forum. AZAPO, the moving spirit behind the NF, launched the organization at a meeting in Hammanskraal, north of Pretoria, in June 1983. The declared purpose was to bring together blacks in opposition to the constitutional proposals, the same dynamic that produced the UDF, but under the banner of Black Consciousness. Over 800 persons representing some 200 organizations reportedly attended. They included several prominent black, Coloured, and Indian leaders—for example, Bishops Desmond Tutu and Manas Buthelezi, Saths Cooper, and

Neville Alexander. The meeting took on racially exclusive and strong socialist tones, which were reflected in the National Forum's manifesto. In stark contrast to the UDF's attempt at a broad, nonracial appeal, the NF manifesto declared opposition to "the system of racial capitalism which holds the people of Azania in bondage for the benefit of the small minority of white capitalists and their allies, the white workers and the reactionary sections of the black middle class." It further called for control by workers of the "means of production, distribution, and exchange" and stated that "the struggle against apartheid is no more than the point of departure for our liberation efforts."

The National Forum has been far less vocal and visible than the UDF. It does not appear to have a permanent organizational structure, and its strident rhetoric has dampened the enthusiasm of its more moderate supporters. Indeed, several have chosen to link themselves informally with both the NF and the UDF but affiliate with neither. While many veteran Black Consciousness stalwarts such as Hlaku Rachidi and Saths Cooper have helped organize the NF, many others (e.g., former AZAPO President Curtis Nkondo) have either joined the UDF or maintained a neutral position. AZAPO remains the NF's most important component but, in recent commemorative meetings and press interviews, AZAPO leaders have not mentioned the NF.

Although the NF has divided some groups (for example, a delegation walked out of the Black Consciousness-based Media Workers' Association of South Africa in January 1984 over the issue of white participation and UDF affiliation), it still has a credible constituency because it represents an important group of mostly young, student-age activists who see themselves as heirs to the Black Consciousness movement and are impatient with the perceived moderate ways of their elders, including the ANC and the UDF. Significantly, the PAC, which shares the NF's philosophy and has been quiescent for so long, seems to be experiencing a modest revival in its influence in Black Consciousness circles.

7. The South African Federal Union (SAFU)

An unexpected entry into the anticonstitution forces was a moderately conservative black coalition initially launched in August 1983 as the Movement for National Unification and later calling itself the South African Federal Union. SAFU is philosophically akin to the now-defunct Black Unity Front and South African Black Alliance led by Chief Buthelezi. Buthelezi played a key role in SAFU's formation, but the impetus for such an organization also came from senior officials of the National African Federated Chamber of Commerce (NAFCOC), a moderate grouping of black entrepreneurs and businessmen with a large national membership and led by the respected banker and businessman Sam Motsuenyane. SAFU includes all the chief ministers and chief executive councillors of the nonindependent homelands, Chief George Matanzima of "independent" Transkei, representatives from the Interdenominational African Ministers' Association of South Africa, and officials from the United Councils Association of South Africa, a group representing municipal councils.

Although SAFU appears to have made little impact so far and faces considerable black animosity because of the homeland connection, its existence in opposition to the constitution and in support of a national convention and "the establishment of a greater South Africa" underscores the extent to which the government's constitutional change has galvanized the black community as a whole.

8. Trade Unions

Black trade unionism has become a new force in recent years — a force that many observers believe could, in the long run, have far greater impact on the rate and direction of change than any or all of the political groups on which attention is now focused. A series of illegal strikes carried out in 1973 by black industrial workers in Durban, followed by a number of government concessions (including new minimum pay scales for urban workers, a limited legal right to strike, and open recognition of the need for more technical training opportunities for black workers) helped set the stage for some watershed events of 1979. These were the publication of the report of the Wiehahn Commission of Inquiry into Labour Legislation and action by parliament to amend the Industrial Conciliation Act to allow black workers to join registered labor unions if they are permitted to live with their families in urban areas. The government by ministerial action later extended this right to commuters and migrants for an indefinite period.

Despite increasing government surveillance and harassment of specific union leaders and unions it perceives to be involved in politics, new unions and union groupings continue to multiply among black workers. In recent years this growth has been phenomenal, with a 200 percent surge in black membership between 1980 and 1983 (from 220,000 to 670,000). The black trade union movement's potential for forcing change on the shop floor, in management attitudes, and in the economic structures of South Africa cannot be underestimated. (See, for example, *Black Trade Unions in South Africa* by David Hauck, published by the Investor Responsibility Research Center, Washington, D.C., in 1982.)

Many unions, taking a long-term view, try to avoid political or quasi-political demands and focus on the immediate priorities of shop floor organization and creation of a national trade union federation to protect rights gained. Most major union groups will speak out on specific issues such as the Industrial Court system or certain broader issues (bannings, detentions, black unity). Others have become actively engaged in the current political groupings. The UDF, the National Forum, and even Inkatha claim some union support. In the case of the UDF, such major trade union groups as the Council of Unions of South Africa (which includes the National Union of Mineworkers), the South African Allied Workers Union, the Motor Assembly and Component Workers Union of South Africa, and the

General and Allied Workers Union have affiliated; in some cases, however, all their member unions may not have been consulted. Several groups, notably the Media Workers' Association of South Africa, have been divided over affiliation.

9. What Lies Ahead?

Although there has been a dramatic convergence of black opinion in South Africa on the constitutional issue, serious divisions remain. The ANC-PAC relationship is reflected in the groups they have ideologically spawned. The UDF publicly denies ANC connections, but openly calls its members "charterists." Although there is no clear evidence of PAC organizational involvement in the National Forum or AZAPO, blacks supporting those groups openly talk of the PAC, and there may be crossover membership.

The PAC's public support of the National Forum was illustrated by PAC Chairman John Pokela's prediction in an interview with *New African* (London, May 1984) when he stated that the NF had "the best chance of succeeding" while the UDF "embraces all shades of multiracialism [and contains] constituents [which are] enemies of the Azanian African majority. . . . " Meanwhile, the ANC's Oliver Tambo, in an interview with the same publication (April 1984), took the position that "the mass opposition of our people . . . united today in the ANC, the UDF, the trade unions, the youth and women's movement without regard to ethnicity, race and color" is throwing the government's plans into "a crisis."

These divisions have other antecedents beyond the historical ANC-PAC relationship. With the PAC in eclipse throughout the 1970s, the ANC had taken on a predominant role as *the* external representative of South Africa's blacks. Black Consciousness advocates and student activists would not dispute that point, but many of them take exception to ANC misrepresentation of certain internal events in the mid-1970s. Student leaders were especially angered in 1976–1977 by ANC claims that the widespread civil protests and resulting clashes with authorities that began in Soweto were orchestrated or inspired by the ANC. Some of this anger was based on ANC-Black Consciousness ideological differences, but it also reflected a human aspiration to be understood and credited properly. In addition, there was concern that the focus on the ANC had the effect of fueling government "Communist onslaught" propaganda, thus allowing Pretoria to sidestep dealing with the specific grievances that precipitated the protests.

We are also witnessing here a syndrome that has recurred again and again among externally based ("exile") political organizations in Africa. The ANC and PAC are both victims of their distance from their constituencies. Although there is little doubt about the ANC's growing presence within South Africa in recent years, it does not necessarily follow that this growth reflects a strong allegiance to the external ANC of Oliver Tambo. Notions of the ANC among blacks within South Africa are often of a resurgent Nelson Mandela and Walter Sisulu. Restrictions on domestic press coverage of banned organizations are, of course, a factor contributing to the limited identification with the less familiar exiled leaders.

In the face of these deep divisions, recent bridge-building successes warrant a closer look. The fact that the motivation for the formation of the UDF, the NF, and the South African Federal Union has been opposition to the current constitutional process rather than any perceived need for reconciling ANC-PAC-Black Consciousness ideologies would seem to be a positive development.

Another straw in the wind is the urging by a significant range of major black leaders of a modus vivendi between the UDF and the National Forum. Dr. Nthato Motlana of Soweto's Committee of Ten and Bishops Desmond Tutu and Manas Buthelezi are among those who have tried to interact with both groups. Several Black Consciousness leaders—including Dr. Mamphela Ramphele, Zwelakhe Sisulu, and Curtis Nkondo—have also attempted to keep the public rhetoric conciliatory. Even Ish Mkhabela of AZAPO has stated: "We do not see divisions among the oppressed. We are one. . . . [The UDF] have their weaknesses and, in the long term, are fraught with dangers and pitfalls [but] AZAPO is prepared to be part of a principled unity with any organization engaged in the struggle." AZAPO's Secretary Muntu Myeza has been quoted in the press as having said that AZAPO was not "in opposition [or] antagonistic" to the UDF because "we all ultimately have the same objective." ⟨Winnie Mandela, a key figure in any unity move, supports the UDF, but is also popular with Black Consciousness. She dismisses the differences between the groups as relatively unimportant and says she is "cheered" by developments, characterizing the constitution as the "best unifying factor" in years for blacks.⟩

Meanwhile, the government has not been idle. The first few months of the UDF's and NF's existence were relatively trouble-free, with a short detention of one UDF official and the banning of several meetings. Monitoring has escalated as these groups have demonstrated more appeal and clout. AZAPO offices and the homes of at least 41 of its members in various parts of the country have been raided. In Johannesburg, documents, typewriters, files, filing cabinets, and other office equipment were confiscated in May 1984.

As its campaign against the elections began to prove effective, the UDF also felt the sting of official sanctions. This began with the arrest of representatives of at least 44 affiliates at an antiapartheid rally in Durban on June 23, 1984, and several other isolated incidents. After the low Coloured turnout for the August 22 poll, but prior to the Indian elections, authorities detained 47 UDF leaders along with 152 others participating in protest actions. Fifteen of those UDF leaders were still being held as of late October 1984 under Section 28 of the Security and Terrorism Act, which is a preventive detention clause allowing for six months detention without charge or legal access.

It appears that the government was initially cautious in its approach to the UDF, possibly wishing to avoid a repetition of the kind of world condemnation that followed the 1977 bannings and detentions of Black Consciousness leadership. The effective election protest of the UDF has hardened the government's attitude, although the detentions appear not to have been universally agreed upon within the cabinet. Many UDF officials and informed observers are openly worried about a possible banning of the organization or, more probably, some of its affiliate groups and key leaders. In the wake of the recent township disturbances, Minister of Law and Order Louis le Grange has stated that the UDF has the "same goals" as the ANC and the South African Communist Party and is "creating a revolutionary climate" in South Africa.

How the government deals with the UDF-NF phenomenon in the months ahead will, of course, dictate to a great extent whether the new sense of shared purpose represented in these organizations can be sustained long enough to confirm the existence of a meaningful political force beyond the limited and transitory objectives that brought so many diverse elements together in 1983 and 1984.

Whatever the future holds, the emergence of national organized political entities, the first since the 1950s, must be regarded as a landmark in South Africa's evolution. Given the heightened politicization of urban (and also homeland) blacks that has resulted from the constitution issue, even moderates are now impelled to speak out, organize, or join alliances in opposition to a new law of the land that ignores their existence.

4

Black Education in South Africa: Key or Chimera?

John A. Marcum

April 1985

Deep currents of social change are welling up beneath the hard surface of white rule in South Africa. Among the most significant of these currents are those developing in black education, which has become a major focus of public debate, protest, and expenditure.

Some skeptics believe that expanded educational opportunity is likely only to reinforce an exploitative order and thereby render ultimate large-scale violence more rather than less probable. In *Apartheid and Education* (Johannesburg: Ravan Press, 1984), Peter Kallaway of the University of Cape Town discounts liberal initiatives for educational reform as a stratagem to build an enlarged black middle class and integrate it into a basically unchanged and iniquitous political-economic system. Education is essentially a dependent variable, he argues, and schooling is a "mechanism of class domination." Constricted by a complicit "technicism" that responds to the demands of the prevailing system, educators focus on producing more vocationally trained manpower without challenging the underlying structures of racial separatism.

Even if one accepts that reform-minded whites in or out of government may seek to serve and preserve their own interests as they perceive them, the education-as-a-control-mechanism argument leaves at least one important question unposed and unanswered. What might be the *unintended consequences* of massively expanded and substantively improved black education?

Sobering Demography

The South African government's newfound interest in black education is rooted in sobering demography. According to the Institute for Futures Research at the University of Stellenbosch, South Africa's population may leap from 28.6 million in 1980 to 45 million in 2000, with whites down from 16 percent to 10 percent of the total. Standing alone, the relatively static white minority of less than 5 million cannot hope to provide the cadres of high-level professional, technical, and managerial manpower necessary for the development and sustenance of a sophisticated modern economy.

This view is shared by the National Manpower Commission established by the government in 1979 to advise on manpower problems and policy. The chair of the Commission, H.J.J. Reynders, was prompt to conclude that "the contradiction of an excess of semiskilled workers accompanied by a shortage of artisans and high-level manpower" meant that labor matters would "come increasingly under the spotlight." In an influential report published in 1981, the Commission warned that there would have to be a dramatic increase in the number of highly educated African engineers, managers, and entrepreneurs as well as skilled workers, artisans, and technicians. Should South Africa attempt instead to rely on the white minority for top-level manpower, such a choice would not "offer all its people an acceptable standard of living," and a "relative deterioration" of the economy could be "expected."

Leadership within the private sector of the South African economy has concurred with the Commission that educational opportunities for blacks must be greatly expanded. Business-oriented publications cite research estimates that between 1977 and 1987 close to 270,000 job hunters will have entered the job market yearly (730 a day) and for the most part will have joined an existing pool of 2.5 million un- and underemployed, even as the shortage of skilled manpower has soared. With a need for some 23,000 artisans and 9,500 technicians annually, as matched against a current output of less than 10,000 and 2,000 respectively, "the technological uplift of black workers via education, training and improved industrial relations" comes to be seen as "the real key to South Africa's future productivity" (*Flying Springbok*, July 1983).

Assessing South Africa's demography from a more disinterested, systemic vantage point, the director of the Institute for Futures Research, Dr. P.H. Spies, stresses that economic advance and social well-being anywhere depend primarily upon the development of human resources. Consequently, a telescoped educational effort that relies heavily upon new technologies represents the only way for South Africa to break out of political and economic rigidities and move into a more flexible mode of social change. Spies argues that it is an enabling process of genuine education, education in which people learn to think independently and systemically, not a quest for constitutional formulas, that may be expected to open the door to human creativity and accommodation.

Much as Nigeria relied on a single source of national wealth (oil) and neglected vital food production, South Africa for many years relied heavily upon gold and neglected development of its human resources. It was only as the price of gold sank from $800 down to $300 an ounce that the country's political leadership began to give serious consideration to the economic consequences of racial policies that left up to 50 percent of the total population (nearly 70 percent of Africans) functionally illiterate. Its imprudence having at least matched that of the Third World leaders it is so quick to criticize, Pretoria only belatedly came to accept the necessity for vastly expanded educational opportunity.

Given the time lost and the bitterness generated as a

result of past policy and continuing political exclusion, even a rapid expansion of black education cannot avoid hostile distrust on the part of many black parents and students and at least a transitional increase in social cleavage within the black community. According to the Institute for Futures Research, remorseless (though "influx-controlled") urban migration may raise the population of South African cities and their black appendages from 13.7 million to about 30 million between 1980 and the year 2000. Although the share of disposable income earned by Africans, Coloureds, and Asians combined may grow from 37 percent to 57 percent of the national total during this same period, over 5 million persons are likely to be left on the margins to live essentially unschooled and un- and underemployed in stark urban and rural poverty.

Apartheid's Educational Dimension

Upon coming to power in 1948, the National Party's Afrikaner leadership began fashioning an educational system based upon strict racial and ethnic compartmentalization. It proceeded to impose upon voteless Africans an atavistic, largely pretechnological "Bantu education" system that focused on ethnic culture and vernacular languages and deemphasized English, mathematics, and science. The most generous interpretation that could be placed on this forced march into parochialism would be that the Afrikaner's own struggle against British domination had conditioned him to believe that Africans too should work out their destiny within the communal framework of ethnolinguistic nationalism. By simultaneously forcing the study of Afrikaans upon African schools, however, the government bared its underlying determination to secure a new era of Afrikaner dominance.

The quality of black education plummeted. At the university level, the government reduced the University College of Fort Hare, the alma mater of most of the country's African intelligentsia, to the status of just one (the Xhosa one) of several ethnic "bush" universities decreed for Africans. At the same time, it barred the door to top-quality higher education at the would-be racially "open" Universities of Witwatersrand and Cape Town. The latter protested but bowed to the government's will and purged themselves of their small (5 to 6 percent) but growing number of African, Coloured, and Asian students.

Standards of instruction in English fell at all levels. The separation of English-language and Afrikaans-language (white) schools lowered the quality of bilingualism in all schools. As English-speakers withdrew from the increasingly Afrikaner-dominated education profession, 70 percent of South Africa's teachers came to be drawn from Afrikaans-language institutions. These teachers, in turn, inflicted their reduced English proficiency (aggravated by a disinclination to use the language) upon African students who were, and still are, obliged to spend their early school years learning in a vernacular language.

Ethnocentric government policies pushed Afrikaans-medium universities ahead of the previously dominant English-language institutions in terms of funding and enrollments, with the latter surging from 8,900 in 1954 to over 51,000 in 1980. Although African school and university enrollments rose, gross underprovision of facilities, libraries, textbooks, and teachers' salaries led to cumulative deficiency and demoralization. Just how formidable and enduring an obstacle to real educational development the legacy of Bantu education remains is evident from government acknowledgment that, as of 1985, some 80 percent of the African teachers upon whom such development would have to depend are themselves educationally underqualified.

The End of Complacency

It was student anger, targeted on obligatory Afrikaans but grounded in pervasive resentment of the whole educational system, that sparked the violent explosion that spread out from the Soweto township near Johannesburg in 1976.

David versus Goliath images of rock-hurling youths bat-
tling motorized police burst onto the screens of television
sets around the world. The magnitude and intensity of the
violence, along with the international revulsion it spawned,
convinced the government that the costs of maintaining the
status quo were untenable. Having already moved some
distance from the crude and narrow (*verkrampte*) stance of
initial Verwoerdian apartheid doctrine toward a more pragmatic form of white hegemony, the government was by this
time quietly relaxing the color bar in some professions and
edging away from the disabling anachronism of Bantu education in response to manpower imperatives. The explosion
of 1976, however, blasted Prime Minister B.J. Vorster's government out of its lingering complacency and embarrassed
even previously indifferent whites into openly accepting a
need for comprehensive educational reform – albeit still
within a framework of communal segregation.

By this time, quantitative as contrasted to qualitative
trends were already on an upswing. According to government statistics (which included the designated ethnic
"homelands" for this period), between 1955 and 1975 African primary school enrollment rose from 970,000 to
3,380,000, secondary school enrollment from 35,000 to
318,000, and university enrollment from approximately 500
to 4,500. Comparable numbers were enrolled in University
of South Africa (UNISA) correspondence courses. Over a
50-year period (1927–1977), the overall distribution of education had changed substantially, down from 53.6 percent
white to 16.4 percent white.

In the late 1970s, the pace of change intensified. Government expenditure on African education (excluding capital expenditure and universities but including homelands)
rose from R68 million in 1972–1973 to R298 million in
1980–1981. This still left the government spending 10
times as much on each white as on each African student,
however, and not all of the statistics were encouraging. In
1980 only 31,000 of the more than 600,000 African children
who had entered school in 1969 reached the last year (stan-

dard 10) of secondary school – a 5 percent completion rate. In 1979, only 1,000 of the over 6,000 students then enrolled at the three universities then ascribed to Africans (Universities of the North, Fort Hare, and Zululand) successfully completed a course of study (generally three years), suggesting a dropout rate of at least 50 percent.

De Lange's Post-Verkrampte Blueprint

In order to help chart its course amidst growing clamor for educational reform, the government, in mid-1980, commissioned a massive study of South African education to be carried out under the auspices of the Human Sciences Research Council (HSRC). A select 25-member multiracial committee headed by the rector of the Rand Afrikaans University (RAU), Dr. J.P. de Lange, mobilized hundreds of researchers for a survey that extended from informal and preschool to graduate education. After a year of intense labor, publicity, and suspense, the committee submitted its report in July 1981.

The de Lange committee recommended substantial changes. These included creation of a single, unified department of education; administrative decentralization, with communal or racial criteria for school admissions to be determined by regional authorities (an innovation intended to open the way to some voluntary integration); compulsory primary education and funding parity for all students, teachers, and schools as quickly as possible; university autonomy over (racial) admissions policies; development of more technical and private-sector education; and establishment of a multiracial Council of Education to oversee implementation of the committee's proposals for comprehensive educational development. These proposals were judged by the black daily *Sowetan* (November 25, 1983) to be capable of profoundly restructuring education and "setting the scene for a new era" in South Africa.

The government's preliminary response was to endorse

a list of hortatory goals/principles set forth by the committee, including "equal opportunities" and "equal standards"
in education for "every inhabitant" of the country, but also
to express some ominous "reservations." The National Party's commitment to education of a "Christian and national"
character taught in a "mother tongue" in separate schools
administered by separate departments for "each population
group" was reaffirmed. Public comment was invited, and
Professor de Lange was asked to head up an interim "working party" to review this comment (some 10,000 pages
in all). "Plodding" is the word that best describes the complex political process that would ultimately determine what
the government could accept of the de Lange committee
recommendations.

In November 1983, two years after publication of the
original committee report, the long-awaited *White Paper on
the Provision of Education in the Republic of South Africa*
was presented to parliament. In response to the proposal
for a single, overarching department of education, the government agreed to lodge "general" responsibility for educational norms and standards, data and support services, salaries and conditions of employment, coordination with
homeland administrations, and budget planning in one cabinet-level post. Reportedly under political pressure from
the conservative education bureaucracy in Transvaal, however, the government stressed that education would remain
a communal or "own" affair, with none of the more than a
dozen ministers of education for separate racial groups and
homelands to report or be considered "subordinate" to the
minister with "general" responsibilities. By rejecting sub-
sumption of continued compartmentalization under a single minister, even if only symbolically, the White Paper
shattered African hopes for a "new era" and drew attention
away from the government's more positive responses to
other de Lange committee recommendations. Later, sensing the cost of this deference to right-wing pressure, the
government decided to lodge "general" responsibilities with
the (white) Department of National Education and claimed
that it had thereby created the central ministry called for

by de Lange. But this gesture was insufficient to dissuade Africans from the bitter conclusion that separate Bantu education, though modified, would persist.

Particularly disappointing to Dr. de Lange was the government's failure to free education from the stifling hold of entrenched bureaucracy and to decentralize its administration within new, socially more responsive, enterprising, and inclusive regional units – a cause that he continues to argue. He hailed, however, new government initiatives to create preschool and adult education opportunities for blacks, establish universal norms for classroom facilities and for teacher qualifications and salaries, and organize upgrading programs for black teachers. Speaking in August 1983 at a USSALEP (United States-South Africa Leader Exchange Program) conference on U.S. initiatives in support of black education in South Africa, de Lange declared himself a long-term optimist and pointed with satisfaction to a rise of 17.1 percent in the 1982–1983 education budget (R3.1 billion, ahead of expenditure on defense for the first time).

Further confirming a propensity to equivocate when confronted with a need to act against its own doctrinal leanings, the government initially declined to grant universities full authority over admissions policy and announced adoption of a racial quota system instead. Then it backed away under pressure from university leaders and agreed not to implement the quota so long as university admissions did not produce sudden or massive shifts in institutional (meaning racial) character. This left self-declared "open" universities free to internalize a process by which they had reopened and built modest but significant African enrollments in the 1970s on the basis of case by case government permission. How far they might be allowed to go and for how long remained in question.

Overall, partially positive inconsistency characterized the government response to de Lange and the education crisis. Pretoria welcomed the advice to expand technical education and agreed in principle to the merit of subsidizing some private education. It had already placed a high priority on the establishment of technikons (racially segregated tertiary polytechnic institutions providing job-oriented instruction in applied sciences, technology, and related skills). And it had permitted a number of private schools, such as St. Barnabas College (Anglican) of Johannesburg, to develop and offer exemplary multiracial education to a limited number of select students; some of St. Barnabas's 300 racially mixed students even lived in as boarders. On the other hand, the government sidestepped the advice that it waive the Group Areas Act in order to permit thousands of students in overcrowded black schools and technical colleges to be accommodated in underutilized white facilities.

Instead of agreeing to form a single, unifying advisory council to oversee implementation of educational development, the government decided to form two: a 20-member South African Council of Education (SACE) representing all population groups to advise on overall policy for school-level education, and a 12-member multiracial Universities and Technikons Advisory Council (UTAC) for higher education. Whether these bodies could develop into effective monitors and catalysts of enlightened policy would depend on the quality and independence of their membership and, once again, on the government's preparedness to heed reasoned counsel.

Unfortunately, the precedents were not overly promising. Despite a now well-seasoned ascendancy over earlier domination by English-speakers and a now inescapable awareness of educational needs, the Botha government remained enmeshed in the contradictions of "separate but equal" dogma and had yet to demonstrate the vision or political self-confidence necessary for bold and unequivocal action.

New Realities in 1985

In 1984 a new constitution adopted in the name of reform granted a parliamentary role and limited political rights to Asian and Coloured minorities but left the African majority of nearly 75 percent in a voteless limbo. Racial polarization intensified and the guarded optimism earlier generated in the field of education by the de Lange committee gave way to pervasive doubt and pessimism.

Within a context of declining economic fortunes, the magnitude of educational need came increasingly to be seen as defying the government's means as well as its will. Illustrative of the scope of this defiance, a 1984 report from the South African Medical Association indicating that 66 percent of African children suffer from protein deficiency buttressed assertions by, among others, the opposition Progressive Federal Party's health spokesman, Dr. Marius Barnard, that high dropout rates among African pupils are related to extensive malnutrition. He cited research showing children with a history of protein deficiency to have a failure rate twice that of a control peer group. Work at the Bureau for Economic Research at Stellenbosch suggested, moreover, that many African children have been permanently handicapped by malnutrition before entering school: physical and mental stunting, hearing and sight defects, and sheer hunger conduce to apathy, low concentration, lack of maturation, low achievement, absenteeism, and ultimately a high dropout rate.

Cognitive difficulties associated with plunging children from traditional, rural societies (69 percent of African schoolgoers live in homelands) into an educational system rooted in a change-oriented, industrial society also pose formidable difficulties. The problems these children experience in understanding the new system, education analyst Elizabeth Dostal recently argued at Stellenbosch's Institute for Futures Research, hamper "logical thinking" and the ability to cope cognitively with daily situations. This phenomenon "is further characterized by imitative behavior and rote (parrot fashion) learning without understanding." Though susceptible of exaggeration, the cultural leap required does clearly place a crucial and intimidating pedagogical burden on underprepared black teachers.

That a truly massive effort will be needed if even marginally acceptable standards are to be realized in black education has been further underscored by recent trends. The number of African secondary school graduates doubled between 1975 and 1978 (5,529 to 11,167), then jumped by a factor of nearly eight by 1984 (83,000), and, according to government projections, may reach 190,000 (outnumbering whites 3 to 1) by the year 2000. Partly because there are simply not enough qualified teachers or adequate instructional materials and facilities to serve these swelling enrollments, the quality of black secondary education has measurably deteriorated. Assessing this deterioration, Kenneth B. Hartshorne of the Center for Continuing Education at the University of Witwatersrand cites low morale as another major contributing factor. African teachers suffer from a demoralizing inability to command respect in the classroom, a plight exacerbated by the student rebellion of 1976. Even worse, they suffer from a debilitating loss of self-respect as a result of working within a system of which they disapprove.

Evidence for a decline in standards is discernible in the sharp fall in the proportion (as distinct from the number) of African students who pass the national matriculation examination at the end of secondary school. Between 1978 and 1982, while the number of successful "matric" examinees rose from 7,468 to 30,541, the proportion of those taking the examination who passed fell from 76 percent to 51 percent. (According to Hartshorne, the foregoing statistics exclude homelands from the time they became independent: Transkei in 1976, Bophuthatswana in 1977, Venda in 1979, and Ciskei in 1981. To the figure of 30,541 passes in 1982, therefore, another 20,000 might be added. According to the South African Institute of Race Relations' *Survey of Race Relations in South Africa, 1983*, only Transkei is excluded from these figures from 1981 on. The discrepancy illustrates the near impossibility of securing clear and comparable data given current homeland policies). Even more devastating, the proportion of those (3,236 in 1978 and 6,336 in 1982) who passed with "exemptions" and thereby qualified for university entrance fell from 33 percent to 11 percent. Of those who passed the matric, more did so by squeaking through with low marks. And reflective of the enduring costs of Bantu education, only 521 of the over 20,000 who graduated from secondary schools in 1981 passed the matric in advanced physical sciences and 1,795 in advanced mathematics.

The Neglected Rural Majority. Rural South Africa confronts government with especially acute, if relatively unpublicized, educational need. Speaking with sweeping acerbity, Oscar Dhlomo, the minister of education for the territorially fragmented KwaZulu homeland of nearly 4 million people, recently described schooling in all the homelands as "glorified literacy campaigns parading as full-fledged educational systems."

In the cases of those homelands declared independent, hundreds of thousands of young people simply evaporate from the revealing columns of South African government educational statistics. Isolated from cultural contact with an external world that refuses to recognize them, the resource-poor "TBVC countries" (Transkei, Bophuthatswana, Venda, and Ciskei) thus risk seeing their children become the forgotten youth of South Africa. For the time being, the South African government does continue to subsidize the general budgets (R553 million in 1982) and thus the modest educational systems of these areas, but in the guise of international assistance through the Department of Foreign Affairs rather than as an accepted domestic responsibility.

Similarly marginal and subject to neglect, nearly 500,000 rural Africans attend over 5,000 farm schools within "white South Africa." The government pays teachers' salaries and prescribes the syllabus but white farmers construct the schools, control admissions, and fix the level of education offered—a system unlikely to accelerate African advance.

Literacy Is Not Enough. To this array of daunting realities must be added the fact that for the foreseeable future the pressing educational need in economic terms will be for

African manpower qualified in precisely the fields and at exactly the levels most difficult of attainment: manpower possessed of the highest technological and managerial skills.

Given low standards and high dropout rates in science and mathematics and the related fact that only about 3 percent of the enrollment in technikons, technical colleges, and universities combined is African, some analysts suggest that South Africa could have a shortage of up to 500,000 persons in these highest skill categories by the year 2000. Such analysis specifically projects a need to bring some 4,300 African, Asian, and Coloured "executives" into the labor market each year, almost 10 times the 1970–1980 average of 490 a year. There will be a comparable need for African university-trained civil engineers – a total of less than 20 have been produced to date.

On the other hand, projections show that as many as a million Africans with general educational experience through standard 8 or 10 (junior high/high school) may find themselves jobless, frustrated by educational preparation judged inadequate or inappropriate for the job market. In a report summarizing research that predicts just such an end-of-the-century predicament, Graham Watts of the Johannesburg *Sunday Express* (October 21, 1984) concluded despairingly: "The keys that unlock the door to the future were lost long ago."

New Financial Constraints. In February 1983, then-Minister of Finance Owen Horwood publicly estimated that realization of racial parity in schooling by 1990 (assuming no inflation) would require an annual education outlay of R5.2 billion, some 40 percent of the government budget. Independently, Dr. A. Roukens de Lange of the Institute for Futures Research has concluded that, in order to equalize per student expenditure among all racial groups (based on a 20 to 1 student-teacher ratio), the government would have to spend some 38 percent of its budget on education. Put in comparative terms, South Africa would thus have to expend some 11 to 13 percent of its gross domestic product (GDP) on education, about twice the amount spent by most Western countries. The finance minister seemed nonetheless to imply that parity was possible if "users" (meaning the private sector as distinct from taxpayers) bore a significant share of the costs. And moves by the Transvaal provincial government to introduce fees in white schools suggest that at least a modest redistributive process may be accepted as a necessary corollary of the effort to expand black education.

Most political analysts, however, incline to the view that, given the state of South Africa's economy, the costs of achieving equal educational opportunity in the near term would be politically prohibitive. The government has set no target date for such an achievement. The goal of equality, researcher A. Roukens de Lange concludes, is fated to remain "a dream for the distant future." White South African parents may be willing to pay modest school fees but they show no sign of being prepared to pay taxes at a level that would substantially lower their standard of living or raise student-teacher ratios in white schools (18.2 to 1 versus 42.7 to 1 in African schools). They continue to decline to share underutilized school facilities, let alone to accept classroom integration, as means for achieving educational parity.

In the face of a serious economic recession, the government has continued to increase incrementally expenditure on African education (rising from R560 million in 1983 to R709 million in 1984, homelands excluded), while it has reduced expenditure in most other areas. But the South African economy is sorely constricted by the depressed price of gold, the devastating multiyear drought, inadequate savings reserves, regional military ventures (an estimated \$1.5 billion in direct military and related economic subsidies for Namibia alone), and an apartheid-bloated bureaucracy variously estimated at 390,000 to 600,000 and said to increase at a rate of 4.5 percent a year (80,000 added so far under P.W. Botha's stewardship). There is considerable doubt that such an economy can bear the costs of an educational reform that must include, for example, training, upgrading, and support for tens of thousands of black teachers.

In the absence of a new white political consensus that would alter priorities and permit a massive mobilization and reorientation of national resources, therefore, rapid qualitative change in black education has come to be seen as an illusory goal by Africans who earlier had allowed their expectations to be raised by proposals and discussions surrounding the labor of the de Lange committee.

Back to the Streets

It was within this context of fallen hopes accompanied by rising unemployment, living costs, and racial antipathy that South African students in 1984 once again mobilized in schools and universities around the country. By late 1984, the press was regularly reporting that over 200,000 students (at a given time) were boycotting classes, roaming the streets in rock-throwing bands, sparking violent demonstrations, and organizing for sustained action through the rival countrywide networks of the (multiracial) Congress of South African Students (COSAS) and the Black Consciousness-oriented Azanian Students' Movement (AZASM).

Nothing the government said or did sufficed to normalize matters. In October 1984, when 7,000 troops entered the East Rand township of Sebokeng to "restore order" and distributed leaflets urging students to return to their classes, the boycott only intensified. At the beginning of the new academic year in January 1985, however, the government seemed to manage at least a punitive, if temporary, "last word." As African students streamed back to classes nationally, the Department of [African] Education and Training announced that stringent economic conditions would not permit it to repair the hundreds of schools burned, gasoline-bombed, or just window-smashed during the unrest of 1984.

The government can still contain, suppress, and punish African protest. But it seems less and less able to channel social forces to its own ends, and no one can predict how many students might be boycotting classes by October 1985. Minister of [African] Cooperation, Development, and Education Gerrit Viljoen could lament publicly that "unless the black population growth rate slows no social service for the black population will ever become comparable to those of other groups." But so long as the government has no legitimacy in African eyes and so long as urbanization and middle-class status have not yet offered sufficient socioeconomic incentives, the prospect is that programs to encourage family planning will be seen and rejected by many Africans as part of an overall effort to perpetuate white rule.

Some Positive Developments

The magnitude of need and the inadequacies of government policy acknowledged, it would be unrealistic to gainsay the significance of the uneven change that is, in fact, beginning to take place in black education. That overall expenditure on African education has risen by a factor of five since 1978 and the ratio of expenditure on white and African pupils has begun to drop (from 10 to 1 down to under 8 to 1) represents a relative gain.

It is even possible to read the statistics concerning matric examination results as encouraging if one views them over the span of the last two decades and hypothesizes that the recent drop in the proportion of those succeeding is largely a transitional problem tied to rapid expansion. In 1960, only 716 Africans took the matric, 128 passed (17.9 percent), and 28 earned university entrance (3.9 percent); in 1983 72,168 took the matric, 34,876 passed (48 percent), and 7,108 earned university entrance (9.8 percent). In 1990, 29,000 Africans are expected to earn university entrance and in 2000 the figure predicted is 65,000.

Beneath these statistical shifts, moreover, lies a devel-

oping factor of enormous potential, the cumulative impact
of independent black initiatives. A growing legion of voluntary organizations unsullied by collaboration within the official administrative system and ranging from local parent
and student groups to national organizations such as the
Council for Black Education and Research is attempting to
influence the trajectory of change in black education. By
articulating interests, formulating priorities, and pressing
demands from within the black community, these groups
hope to realize informally some small measure of the influence on educational policy denied to them by virtue of African exclusion from the national political process.

Open Universities. In higher education, the initiative
remains overwhelmingly in white hands, although increasing African demand (but not yet organized African leadership) is becoming an important catalyst at the university
level. White universities are now opening their doors, African universities are developing, and African enrollment is
for the first time becoming more than a negligible proportion of the total enrollment of residential universities and
UNISA correspondence programs.

Participation by white institutions in the opening process varies widely. The Universities of Witwatersrand and
Cape Town have undertaken to build solid academic support programs in order to improve the success rate of their
growing number of African, Asian, and Coloured students
(roughly 15 percent of total enrollment). It may be the faculty of the less renowned Pietermaritzburg campus of the
University of Natal, however, that is moving most imagina-
tively and deliberately toward the ultimate goal of convert-
ing a predominantly white institution into an open university with a majority of black students. With administrative
support and some private seed money, it is pioneering in
the development of special instructor-intensive introducto-
ry courses in "Learning, Language, and Logic." Along with
extended efforts in remedial mathematics, these pilot offer-
ings stressing reading and writing in English are being
monitored by other institutions as potentially worthy of

emulation. The inevitably increasing need for special funding promises to be a major concern.

By contrast, the language barrier will probably limit African enrollments at Afrikaans-medium institutions, such as Rand Afrikaans University, that have now declared themselves "open." Such enrollments may be further circumscribed by the persistence of racial prejudice. In a recent referendum at Stellenbosch University, for example, a majority of the 12,000-member student body (which now includes approximately 180 Afrikaans-speaking Coloured students) voted down a proposal to permit construction of a dormitory to house Coloured students on campus.

Vista University. Though laudable and promising for the long run, the gradual opening of white universities cannot possibly meet the soaring African demand for higher education. With this in mind, the government in 1981 created a new, more accessible form of higher education for urban blacks. Critics denounce it as a latter-day version of Bantu education, while enthusiasts hail it as an innovative breakthrough. It takes the form of a stripped-down (makeshift facilities, no sports or extracurricular activities), multicampus (five cities), live-at-home, inexpensive (R153 plus books for a nine-month term), job-oriented (teacher training and commerce) institution known as Vista University. Under a founding rector, C.F. Crouse, seasoned at South Africa's extraordinary "distance learning" university, UNISA, Vista adopted its own entrance examinations (no matric required) and designed a pedagogical format built around study manuals, discussion groups (instead of lectures), tutoring, and frequent testing. From the outset, Vista strictly regulated student organizations, and its relatively mature (average age mid-20s), highly dispersed, career-concerned students were largely nonparticipants in the school unrest of 1984.

As with all institutions of higher learning for Africans, Vista must compete at a disadvantage with predominantly white counterparts in recruiting faculty from a depleted pool of qualified academics. The severe scarcity of science instructors, along with the absence of laboratory facilities, has delayed development of a Vista science curriculum. Even so, the chair of the Vista University Council, RAU's J.P. de Lange, affirms that Vista has managed to attract able faculty from among young, mostly white, urban academics prepared to begin their careers in nearby black institutions (but not in the rural isolation of homeland universities).

Inevitably, Vista suffers from the stigma of being a white-run "apartheid institution" located but not based in (in the sense of being responsible to) the local community. The standards of its instruction and the value of its degrees have yet to be proven. But Vista has been undeniably successful in attracting and holding students. It began in 1985 with 10,000. Its goal is 40,000 within 15 years.

Medical Education. Near to Pretoria and Ga-Rankuwa [township] Hospital, the government has established another all-black (except for postgraduate studies) institution, the Medical University of Southern Africa, or Medunsa. Well-equipped and competently staffed, Medunsa graduated a total of 125 African physicians in its first three classes (1982–1984) and thereby swelled the ranks of the 300-odd African doctors until then practicing in the country. It expects to graduate 600 medical professionals a year when in full operation—physicians (200), dentists, veterinarians, and medical technicians.

Along with the older African-Asian medical school at the University of Natal, Medunsa confronts dramatic need. According to government statistics, one in every 330 whites in South Africa is a physician, while the corresponding figure for Africans, including all homelands, is one in 90,000 (*Panorama*, October 1984). The country's first-ever African veterinarians are scheduled to graduate in 1987. But the cost, approximately R3,500 a year in fees and expenses, is too high for many Africans. It is reported that 30 to 50 of the 120 candidates selected for admission to Medunsa's initial class were unable to enroll for financial reasons.

The Homeland Universities. Leading African academics such as Rector A.C. Nkabinde and Professor Absalom

Vilakazi of the University of Zululand are trying to infuse African residential universities with a sense of identity, legitimacy, and achievement. But they confront enormous odds.

Internally, their institutions are painfully short of African faculty and staff. They must depend largely on available whites. The qualitative implications of this dependency must be seen in the context of the government's policy of installing universities in every homeland from Qwaqwa to KwaZulu – seven so far. Classrooms and administrative offices are dominated by whites (mostly Afrikaners), many of whom resent not having made it into a more prestigious (white) university. Attitudes of paternalistic condescension suffuse the "bush" campuses, alienating students. At Fort Hare, for instance, students complain that faculty are indifferent to their needs, resort to reading aloud from texts in class, and build their lives around midweek shopping excursions to East London. Such negative atmospherics combine with high academic failure rates deriving from inadequate preparation and remediation to reduce students' perceived stakes in their studies. All this fosters a pattern of tension, protest, and dismissal that annually interrupts or terminates the educational careers of thousands of university students.

Externally, the propensity of politically insecure homeland administrations to overreact and intervene against campus critics and "radicals" further compromises efforts to develop these institutions into genuine universities. In 1984, Alan Pifer, president emeritus of the Carnegie Corporation, advised a University of Cape Town convocation: "If a society wishes to gain the full benefits of having an authentic university in its midst, it must respect the institution's independence and integrity." This basic truth was ignored by Chief Kaiser Matanzima of Transkei in 1984, when he destroyed hitherto promising prospects for the development of a serious, community-based institution by firing "subversive" faculty and closing the monumental edifices of the University of Transkei.

Among the homeland universities, only the University of Bophuthatswana (UNIBO) has not been afflicted by chronic unrest and prolonged closures. Under the less intrusive, relatively enlightened administration of Bophuthatswana's president, Chief Lucas Mangope, UNIBO has purposefully recruited and sustained spirited faculty with a "land grant college" commitment to community development.

The importance of institutional independence to intellectual quality has been highlighted by positive response to the elevation of the (predominantly Indian) University of Durban-Westville and the University of Western Cape (UWC) to "autonomous" status in 1984. In a report headed "UWC has broken apartheid's shackles," the Cape *Argus* (October 13, 1984) welcomed the rapidly growing (33 percent increase in 1984), 6,000-student, formerly ascriptively Coloured, now voluntarily community-service-oriented University of Western Cape to the ranks of South Africa's open universities. Under founding Rector Richard van der Ross, UWC has invested heavily in computer-aided remediation and instruction. It has attracted and upgraded an improving faculty that includes such notables as development economist Wolfgang Thomas (a victim of the University of Transkei purge), and supports a lively resource center for improvement of science and mathematics instruction in Coloured, African, and Asian schools of the Cape region.

The Universities of Western Cape and Durban-Westville have now accepted the daunting burden of raising some 15 percent of their funding from private sources, the price of being removed from direct government supervision. It is a price still beyond the financial reach of the homeland universities. Until material and political circumstances enable them too to realize de facto, if not de jure, autonomy, they are fated to function under an apartheid cloud.

If one intended consequence of increasing opportunities for residential university studies is the production of a pliant, apolitical black elite, government policy shows little sign of succeeding. Whether despite or because of severe administrative control over all political activity, student attitudes on African campuses are characterized by high levels of racial sensitivity and political awareness. A survey and analysis of student opinion at five homeland universities by political scientist Gerhard Tötemeyer (*The African University in a Divided Society*, Umtata, 1984) reveals a keen sense of self-identification with South African, not homeland, citizenship, and admiration for such African leaders as Nelson Mandela and Zimbabwe's Robert Mugabe. It also records generally unfavorable views of the Soviet Union and Marxist ideology. At the Universities of Fort Hare and Transkei in the Eastern Cape, on the other hand, the Soviet Union commands considerable respect for its known support of African liberation movements whereas the United States is widely criticized for "selfish accommodation" with South Africa's racial order. The high unemployment rate and long tradition of black political activism in the Eastern Cape doubtless contribute to these differences.

Primary and Secondary Education. Africans who accept office within "apartheid institutions" such as township councils are increasingly subject to social ostracism and even physical assault as "collaborators." At the same time, some of their critics organized in voluntary associations have been winning government recognition and even some policy concessions.

Albeit in an uneasy, uneven, and awkward fashion, Afrikaner leadership has begun to accept the limits of coercive power and thus the necessity to consult and even to negotiate with community-legitimated black leadership. Just as white South Africa is accommodating to collective bargaining by burgeoning black trade unions, so too it seems resigned to dealing with organized parents, teachers, and students. But this interaction can continue and develop only if the political climate does not deteriorate to the point where respected black community leaders feel obliged to cut off contact and conversation with public authorities in order to avoid being labeled and treated as collaborators.

In the midst of massive school boycotts and protests in

1984, Minister of Cooperation, Development, and Education Viljoen acknowledged publicly that black resentment would persist until disparities between white and black education were largely eliminated. Pledging to do his "utmost to eliminate those disparities," Viljoen and his department began to respond to African calls for reform with limited concessions reminiscent of the government's response to the de Lange committee recommendations. He accepted COSAS demands for elected Student Representative Councils (SRCs) in secondary schools—though as a means for improving "communications," not for asserting student responsibilities (as per COSAS proposals). He proposed to create a pyramid of advisory councils that would draw upon voluntary school committees and parent and teacher associations to provide African input into educational planning and policy up to the "highest level." Viljoen and his colleagues also undertook to assure agitated African opinion that they were seriously addressing a wide range of grievances articulated variously by parents, students, and teachers—including excessive corporal punishment and teacher misconduct in the classroom, inflexibility of age limits placed on students, shortages of free and low-cost textbooks, and the paucity of well-trained African circuit inspectors and school administrators as well as teachers.

The value of working with or through black community organizations has also impressed itself on the private sector. A Mobil Oil Corporation seed grant of R450,000 recently sparked the creation of Teacher Opportunities Programmes (TOPS) to improve the quality of teaching in black schools. Unabashedly linked to the "survival of free enterprise in South Africa," TOPS, through more than a dozen regional centers, is now providing off-hours, professional training in substance (English, science, mathematics), teaching methods, and management skills to underqualified teachers, over 1,300 so far. TOPS advertises for contributions from business, arguing that "private enterprise has a crucial role to play because we know that unless our Black pupils are given a solid foundation, we will be doing remedial tasks in education forever."

From the outset, TOPS has also sought to involve teacher associations actively within its programs. Illustrative of how such participation is being used to strengthen black organizational capacity, the TOPS-associated Center for Continuing Education of the University of Witwatersrand recently handed over implementation of the English language upgrading program for teachers in Soweto to the local African Teachers' Association. Such devolution gives black organizations something tangible to deliver to their members and broadens their administrative experience.

Indicative of African determination to initiate and not just participate, a new black organization called Educational Catalysts in Southern Africa (ECSA) headed by businessman Bogie M.H. Mabogoane organized a November 1984 seminar in Johannesburg on the role of sometimes misdirected private sector assistance to black secondary education. Led off by the editor of the influential *Financial Mail*, the seminar bore in on how such assistance might be converted into a positive factor "for achievement and self-pride among pupils in particular and the black community in general."

With the objective of concerting the activities of the growing number of black educational organizations that have emerged in recent years, black leaders created an umbrella Education Coordinating Council of South Africa (ECCSA) in 1982. ECCSA endeavors to bring greater cohesion to the activities of such groups as (1) the South African Committee for Higher Education (SACHED; director, John Samuel), a multicentered purveyor of community-based education in basic skills, teacher upgrading, university preparation or "bridging," and "distance learning" (Turret Correspondence College); (2) the Council for Black Education and Research (chair, Es'kia Mphahlele, professor of literature, University of Witwatersrand), which focuses on cultural discourse, development of black priorities for educational development, and dissemination of both through a quarterly, *Education Press*, and monograph series, *Capricorn Papers*; (3) the Educational Opportunities Council (Bishop Desmond Tutu, chair of trustees, and Dr. Mokgethi B.G. Motlhabi, director), responsible for the selection and subsequent career placement of black graduate and undergraduate students studying for science, mathematics, economics, and other degrees under the South African Education Program (SAEP) in the United States (see "The American Role," below); and (4) other organizations such as the Zingisa Educational Project (Ciskei) and a black Teachers' Action Committee.

Under the leadership of the director of SACHED's Cape Town Center, Dr. Neville Alexander (an alumnus of Robben Island), ECCSA has set as its top priority for black education a national campaign to further the teaching of English as a (unifying) second language. Eschewing a separate budget or bureaucracy, ECCSA hopes to encourage black cultural unity, drawing inspiration from the cultural cohesion and enterprise that so effectively served the Afrikaner. In the words of one activist, "We must beat them at their own game." It also hopes to foster a concerted approach to issues of rural and preschool education, working closely with churches, teachers, and rural associations to build a broad community support base.

Parallel to these efforts to generate so much momentum behind black assertion in education that the government will be forced to come to terms with it, a major debate is emerging within black leadership over general strategy. In the "congress tradition" of multiracial mass action, COSAS and other United Democratic Front organizations argue for combining the elaboration of an all-encompassing Education Charter with widespread protest and boycotts such as those which saw hundreds of thousands of school and university students forsake classes during much of 1984. Though costly to those whose educational careers are interrupted or cut short, this strategy is advocated as part of a larger campaign of open-ended pressure that includes mass meetings, labor stoppages, and boycotts of township elections. Its supporters hope that over time it will undermine government capacity and resolve.

A competing Black Consciousness-oriented approach known as the "Cape strategy" is attracting support among those such as the Azanian Students' Movement who believe that black interests will be better served by following a strategy built around precise goals, short but concerted boycotts, and less dramatic efforts to build up organization and generate leadership. This strategy, which draws its inspiration from experience in the Western Cape, would rely, for example, on boycotts of a day or two accompanied by alternative outside classes (e.g., African history) and student involvement in a range of community preschool or adult education projects. The objective: to demonstrate and build power but not to deprive students of a continuity of education.

Hapless black school teachers and principals are destined to be caught in the middle between these contending strategies on the one hand and government blandishments (higher salaries) and demands/sanctions on the other. Their conflict management and survival skills as well as their educational commitment will be sorely tested if their roles and circumstances are increasingly politicized.

The Political Core of the Issue

In the final analysis, the effectiveness with which Africans are able to capitalize on the intended and unintended opportunities inherent in the expansion of black education will necessarily be a matter of political as well as educational significance. The imaginativeness of leadership, appropriateness of strategies, and discipline of organization will factor heavily in determining the degree of success of black efforts to exploit the chinks in white armor, though realism suggests that education alone cannot provide sufficient black leverage to alter the configuration of power.

An observation recently made by columnist Flora Lewis about the Soviet Union is also applicable to the apartheid system: "Nobody can know the possibilities of evolution and reform in the ... system, its ultimate limits, without testing and challenging it." It may be that the South African system and those heading it will prove resolutely and fatally inflexible and reactive. Or it may be, as Professor de Lange believes, that the basic trend in South Africa is toward "the devolution of power" and an expansion of private enterprise; that resourceful use of new technology — computers, video, educational television — will render a telescoped development of black education feasible even in a time of economic stringency; and that by the time of South Africa's next economic upswing an increased number of literate homes and a sharp rise in skill levels will enable South African blacks to attain an unprecedented level of social well-being. In either case, the expansion of black educational opportunity cannot but test and challenge fundamental structures of the South African system.

Professor de Lange has implied as much in commenting to the press: "We are creating a time bomb if we go on providing education and don't create a situation in which that education can be used." A situation in which that education can be fully used must presumably be a peaceable one of high social mobility possible only in a context of white-black political accommodation. The achievement of such accommodation, therefore, becomes an ever more urgent necessity as black education develops. It will require white (as well as black) leadership marked by moral courage and vision.

The American Role

In 1981, a USSALEP-sponsored team of U.S. educators made a series of recommendations on the ways in which U.S. assistance might play an important catalytic role after concluding an in-country exploration of black education in

South Africa. These recommendations focused on initiatives that emphasize promotion of social justice, seek maximum impact via multiplier effects, replicability, and validation, demonstrate sensitivity to community needs, and reinforce local projects and structures by channeling assistance through and to appropriate private associations. (For the full report, see John A. Marcum, *Education, Race, and Social Change in South Africa*, Berkeley: University of California Press, 1982).

A growing number of creative private and public U.S. undertakings conform harmoniously with these principles. They include Rockefeller Foundation seed grants to a variety of community-generated educational projects; a multiyear USSALEP-Boston University workshop for black journalists; and Ford Foundation support for SACHED-University of Indiana collaboration aimed at establishing a yearlong university preparation program for black students.

In a unique private-public partnership, U.S. university, foundation, and corporate funding ($3 million a year) has been joined by bipartisan congressional funding ($4 million a year) for the South African Education Program (SAEP), which functions on a basis of administrative collaboration between the Educational Opportunities Council in South Africa and the Institute of International Education in New York. Over 200 students were attending universities in the United States under SAEP in January 1985. After a longer than anticipated period of difficult and sensitizing exploration, it now seems possible that agreement may also be reached upon an appropriate mechanism through which to provide AID-funded scholarships to additional hundreds of black students for university-level study within South Africa.

Other educational needs for which U.S. assistance might be effectively tailored include advanced studies and workshops for university and school administrators designed to enhance the independence and competence of their administrations; help in fashioning and implementing more imaginative programs for the advancement of black managers and executives within the private sector (including communication and negotiation skills); and substantial, multiyear funding for a diverse range of community-founded and -based educational programs, helping them to experiment with agendas, methods, and structures of their own making.

Wisely conceived, U.S. assistance can be congruent with black aspirations—that is, with the ardent desire of blacks for education keyed to the development of all dimensions of the human potential. As a catalyst, it need not imply long-term dependency, let alone the chimera of external salvation. For example, the first enterprising returnees from SAEP university studies in the United States have already formed an active alumni association with a self-help orientation. Carefully targeted and sensitively channeled, therefore, assistance to black education offers Americans a feasible and politically acceptable way in which to respond to the moral challenge of South African apartheid.

5

Destabilization and Dialogue: South Africa's Emergence as a Regional Superpower

John de St. Jorre

April 1984

Dialogue, if not eternal friendship, is suddenly the name of the game in southern Africa. And just as South Africans not so long ago were doing most of the fighting, now they are doing most of the talking. A South African-Mozambican "nonaggression and good neighborliness" accord has been signed. South African and Zimbabwean officials deal regularly and amicably on security and economic matters, although Harare has thus far declined to upgrade the relationship to ministerial level. South African and Angolan military personnel are jointly monitoring the former's pledged withdrawal from southern Angola, an exercise that has already involved some jointly administered punishment of recalcitrant South West Africa People's Organization (SWAPO) guerrillas. South African military intelligence has met with senior SWAPO leaders at least once. And there are reports from Western diplomatic sources (unconfirmed by the parties involved) that South African officials have met with top exile leaders of the African National Congress (ANC) in Lusaka. The pivotal questions are why, how far will it go, and do we stand on the brink of a new era of stability and cooperation or is this merely a breathing space before the next round of regional violence?

But first a scorecard. South Africa, without a shadow

of doubt, has notched up a major victory both for its tactics of destabilization and for its long-held strategy of dealing directly, at the highest possible level, with black African governments. The ANC has suffered a severe setback. SWAPO has also lost ground, physically in the cease-fire zone in southern Angola, and politically since it fears that the diplomatic initiative will run out of steam, leaving South Africa more entrenched in Namibia than ever.

The Soviet Union too has registered a setback, more pronounced perhaps in Angola (where it had placed new weaponry — and thus its credibility — on the line in 1983) than in Mozambique. The Front Line states, as a group, have had to genuflect, with varying degrees of grace, to the regional superpower. Further afield, liberal and radical supporters of southern African liberation movements have been stunned and confused, while right-wingers have denounced what they believe is a sellout of pro-Western resistance forces in Mozambique and Angola. The other members of the Western "Contact Group" that has played a leading role since 1977 in the Namibian negotiations — Britain, France, West Germany, and Canada — have had to sit on the fence as their fifth partner, the United States, conducts a nimble if nervous diplomacy. The results so far have strengthened the credibility of Assistant Secretary of State for African Affairs Chester Crocker's policy of "constructive engagement."

It has been South Africa rather than the United States, however, which has provided the dynamic force behind these remarkable events. And South Africa's achievement should be set in its historical context as part of a long-term strategy of reaching outward into Africa and establishing dialogue and détente with black states.

The Historical Backdrop

In a sense, the story begins with the police killings of unarmed black protesters at Sharpeville in 1960, which ushered in a period of domestic unrest and increasing international rejection of South Africa. The government initially responded by turning inward and focusing on what has been called by analysts of the period "the politics of security."

By the time B.J. Vorster became prime minister in 1966, internal violence had been brought under control and white confidence restored. Vorster undertook to rebuild South Africa's foreign relations, with particular attention to the goal of rapprochement with the rest of Africa. In 1967 diplomatic links were established with Malawi, still the only internationally recognized African country to have such relations with South Africa. Two years later came the renegotiation of the 1909 customs union agreement with the former British High Commission Territories of Botswana, Lesotho, and Swaziland. Meanwhile, nonpolitical (sometimes semiclandestine) functional links with black-ruled states were on the rise. In 1970, South Africa offered nonaggression pacts to neighboring black states; these agreements would have inter alia denied facilities to anti-Pretoria dissident movements, but there were no takers.

In September 1974, Vorster reportedly met with the presidents of Senegal and the Ivory Coast during a trip to the latter country. This was followed by a February 1975 meeting with Liberia's president in Monrovia. Later in the same year, Vorster had a highly publicized summit meeting with President Kenneth Kaunda of Zambia and the two countries made a joint effort to resolve the Rhodesian war. Their Rhodesian peace initiative collapsed (owing mainly to intransigence on the part of the Smith regime), and South Africa's ill-fated military intervention in the Angolan civil war was condemned by black African states. By the end of 1975, Pretoria found itself back in the laager, at least as far as aboveboard connections with black Africa were concerned.

Seeing itself alone against the world and the target of a "total onslaught" orchestrated by the Soviet Union, Pretoria countered beginning in 1981 with its own "total strategy." Prime Minister P.W. Botha, much influenced by the military men he had brought with him into the inner circles of government from his 14 years as minister of defense (and by Israeli regional strategy under Prime Minister Menachem Begin), launched a systematic policy of destabilization against his neighbors. The aim was to enfeeble the ANC and SWAPO and strengthen South Africa's military, political, and economic hegemony over the region.

The subtle, behind-the-scenes diplomacy that had characterized South Africa's previous dealings with African countries was swept away, and Foreign Minister Pik Botha and his team of skilled diplomats were sidelined. Washington's privately communicated words of concern and caution were overridden as the military proceeded to occupy parts of southern Angola, raid Lesotho and Mozambique in retaliation for ANC operations believed to have been launched from bases in these countries, and provide various forms of support and encouragement to dissident movements in states perceived to be contributing to the "destabilization" of South Africa or Namibia. Pretoria stopped short, however, of toppling any governments in the region.

There is no doubt that the strategy has worked — helped, of course, by a range of natural disasters (drought, cyclone, flood), the world recession, and the inept economic policies of the targeted states. Bolstered by Prime Minister Botha's impressive victory in the November 1983 constitutional referendum, which revealed a lower ceiling on the strength of Afrikanerdom's right wing than had been previously feared, Pretoria has now moved with enthusiasm into the second phase of what *The Economist* calls its "thump-and-talk" strategy. A tour of the region will help illuminate the dimensions and success of the strategy and provide some tentative pointers for the future.

1. Mozambique

The signing of a "nonaggression and good neighborliness" pact by President Samora Machel and Prime Minister Botha on the banks of the Nkomati River on March 16, 1984 was a signal triumph for South Africa. For both sides, the most important parts of the agreement are the security clauses which pledge an end to South African assistance to the dissident Resistência Nacional Moçambicana (MNR) and a considerable curbing of ANC activities in Mozambique. A joint commission to implement the security agreement was established. As a gesture of goodwill, South Africa agreed to close down the MNR radio station that had been operating from the Transvaal. The Mozambican government, on its part, raided the homes of several prominent ANC members in Maputo on March 24–25, confiscating weapons and making four arrests.

Even so, there are likely to be difficulties in administering the security agreement, since each party may be asking the other for more than it can deliver. The South African government has a list of ANC activists it wants removed from Maputo, the most important being Joe Slovo, a white Johannesburg lawyer who it believes is the ANC's military mastermind, while the Mozambicans want 3,000 MNR activists and supporters repatriated from South Africa. The common border is porous and neither the MNR nor the ANC has shown any intention of playing by the new rules.

Mozambique is also interested in a range of economic benefits that it perceives to be part of the Nkomati package—the revival of trade, renewed use of Maputo's port, increased sales of hydroelectric power from the Cabora Bassa dam to South Africa, and the revival of South African tourism. Implementation will depend not only on how well the security arrangements go, but also on the developmental and budgetary aid that Mozambique so desperately needs.

The Nkomati Accord, while not quite a southern "Camp David," was accorded the drama and symbolism of an elaborate signing ceremony, with Machel, in field marshal's uniform, shaking hands and exchanging gold pens with Botha. Why did one of Africa's most revolutionary states, born of a long guerrilla struggle and imbued with strong Marxist beliefs, conduct such an about-face? The short answer is that Machel had no alternative. Virtually every known natural and man-made disaster has struck Mozambique: drought, cyclone, flood, botched social and economic policies, a chronic shortage of skilled manpower (ever since the Portuguese left en masse at independence in 1975), a drop in world prices for the country's agricultural exports, and a cancerous armed rebellion, backed by South Africa, that threatened the survival of the government.

Before turning to the South African option, Machel sought help from a range of other sources. He went to Moscow in early 1983 to talk to his Soviet friends, but they replied that they could afford no more than they were already giving (arms, heavy machinery, fuel, and some food). An October 1983 tour of Western Europe was a personal triumph, but produced little of substance. Portugal, the former colonial power, was ready in principle to play the lead role in Mozambique's rehabilitation, but is cash-short itself. The Cubans were a possibility, but South Africa made it very clear that it would not permit a Cuban presence on terrain so close to its own.

That left the United States. Relations had reached rock bottom shortly after President Reagan took office, when four members of the U.S. Embassy in Maputo were expelled as alleged spies. The Mozambicans give much of the credit for the warming of relations in the past two years to the personal diplomacy of Frank Wisner, Crocker's principal deputy. The improvement has been symbolized by the return of U.S. representation in the country to ambassadorial status and the appointment of an experienced Portuguese-speaking career officer to the post; meanwhile, Mozambique's first-ever ambassador to the United States has taken up his duties in Washington. But aid from the United States had a price. Maputo would have to mend its fences with South Africa (in effect, loosen its ties with Moscow) before any administration could get Congress to lift the ban imposed on aid to Mozambique in 1976. The Frente de Libertação de Moçambique (FRELIMO), the ruling party, debated and agonized over its limited choices and finally decided to open a serious dialogue with South Africa.

It seems to be a characteristic of Machel and his party

that once a decision is made, even though it may constitute a 180-degree turn, it is implemented with gusto. FRELIMO officials stress that the movement has been at war for 20 years, first against the Portuguese, then against the Rhodesians, and finally against South Africa. The time has come, they argue, for peace and stability—even if the price is supping with the devil. They also emphasize that they have not sold out their revolutionary principles or the ANC. The Nkomati Accord, they say, is not an international treaty since Mozambique does not, and while apartheid remains will not, have diplomatic relations with South Africa. Mozambique will continue to give diplomatic and political recognition to the ANC and the movement will be allowed to maintain offices in Maputo. A week before the signing of the accord, Maputo radio explained the seeming contradictions: "One does not sign a nonaggression pact with one's friends . . . as long as apartheid exists, Mozambique cannot have friendly relations with South Africa, but we can have, and we intend to have, good neighborly relations with South Africa. One can choose one's friends, but not one's neighbors."

Machel was careful to consult with his Front Line neighbors at all stages of the turnaround, and has been adept at mitigating the damage perceived to be done to the pan-African crusade against apartheid. The ANC, which rightly views the pact as a serious setback to its capacity to wage guerrilla and sabotage campaigns against South Africa, has been less understanding. The Soviet ambassador, making the best of a situation generally interpreted as a setback, made a diplomatic speech of "understanding and solidarity" after it was clear that President Machel was determined to establish a new relationship with South Africa.

2. Zimbabwe

Although Zimbabwe's uneasy relationship with its powerful southern neighbor has not changed in any visible way since the "talk" phase of Pretoria's regional policy began, the sudden spurt of dialogue and pact-signing in the region has sent tremors of anxiety through Harare. Zimbabwean officials are concerned about pressure from opposite poles — from the Organization of African Unity (particularly its more radical members) in search of new external bases for the liberation cause in South Africa, and from a South Africa flushed with success in Mozambique pressing for a similar nonaggression accord with Zimbabwe. Neither of these fears seems likely to materialize in the immediate future, but that does not prevent officials in Harare from worrying all the same.

Objectively speaking, South Africa has already achieved most of its policy goals in Zimbabwe. It has known for some time that Prime Minister Robert Mugabe is as good as his word when he says that he is not helping the ANC. Zimbabwean security officials (usually white) have regular meetings with their South African counterparts, either at the border or in South Africa. There is a "hot-line" arrangement for emergencies. South Africa has a large trade mission in Harare headed by a senior Department of Foreign Affairs diplomat; although not recognized as such, the mission performs many of the functions of a normal embassy, including political reporting. The economic hold on Zimbabwe is powerful and can easily be tightened, as a petrol squeeze during Christmas 1982 demonstrated.

Even so, Zimbabwe remains a thorn in South Africa's side. Pretoria resents the steady flow of antiapartheid rhetoric that comes from the officially controlled media in Harare, rhetoric that the Botha government claims "verbally destabilizes" South Africa. It resents Prime Minister Mugabe's refusal to deal at a ministerial level — as Mozambique, Angola, and all the other Front Line states do. It resents Mugabe himself. "The South Africans, rationally, can get along with Mugabe," said a Western diplomat in Harare recently, "but emotionally they would like to get rid of him."

This uneasiness about Mugabe has led Pretoria to invest in a little destabilization insurance through low-level support for the "Super-ZAPU" dissidents in Zimbabwe's Matabeleland. Diplomatic and government sources in Harare assess South African support to consist of occasional assignments of arms, cash, and vehicles for dissidents, as well as assistance for the insurgents' "Radio Truth," which broadcasts regularly to Zimbabwe in Shona, Sindebele, and English from the Transvaal.

3. Angola and Namibia

This is the most complex and uncertain part of the new black and white dialogue in southern Africa. It is also the most difficult for South Africa because, unlike the relationships with Zimbabwe and Mozambique, potentially high costs and risks are involved whichever way the present scenario turns out. There are three phases in the scenario:

The first phase is a military disengagement in southern Angola in which South African forces are to withdraw to the Namibian side of the border. An accord drawn up by the Angolan and South African governments, meeting in Lusaka in mid-February under the chairmanship of President Kenneth Kaunda, established a Joint Monitoring Commission to implement the withdrawal. The South African withdrawal from Angola, which is to take place in four stages, is going more slowly than anticipated and has been complicated by groups of SWAPO insurgents continuing to infiltrate through or around the disengagement area into Namibia. But well-sourced reports of Angolan and South African forces jointly clashing with SWAPO suggest that a measure of trust has been established between the two former enemies. SWAPO's president, Sam Nujoma, has said that he will abide by the cease-fire in Angola but stresses that the struggle will continue inside Namibia until a parallel cease-fire between South Africa and SWAPO is negotiated and signed.

Likewise, Jonas Savimbi, whose União Nacional para a Independência Total de Angola (UNITA) forces have been fighting a guerrilla war against the Luanda government since 1975, has agreed not to interfere in the disengagement zone, but makes it clear that UNITA's war against the Movimento Popular de Libertação de Angola (MPLA) government will continue. In a March 30 news conference in his "provisional capital" of Jamba, Savimbi warned that if UNITA were not accommodated in the Namibia negotiations, regional peace and stability would not be secured: "If the Cubans are sent packing from Angola, Namibia shall henceforth be free. . . . However, as long as MPLA fears UNITA, the Cubans will not leave Angola. Therefore, the independence of Namibia depends upon a direct dialogue between UNITA and MPLA." Meanwhile, the United States, through a small team based in Windhoek, is playing an as-needed mediating role in the relationship between the South African and Angolan forces.

The second phase involves a complicated and delicate set of negotiations in which U.S. diplomacy again comes into play. Two hard decisions will have to be made, one by Angola and the other by South Africa. President José Eduardo dos Santos will have to decide whether he can dispense with the bulk of the Cuban combat forces and Prime Minister Botha will have to bite the bullet on the Namibian independence issue.

Hopes for this phase of the scenario are based on the benefits it offers both sides. For Angola there will be the removal of the South African Defense Force (SADF) beyond the Orange River border with Namibia, a cutoff of aid to Savimbi, the prospect of a new and friendly black state next door in Namibia, diplomatic relations with the United States with the prospect of aid to follow, and an opportunity to rebuild a shattered economy with Western help. For South Africa, there will be an end to the monetary and human cost of protecting Namibia; a removal of a major bone of contention in its relations with the West, Africa, and the international community; and an opportunity to concentrate its time and resources on pressing domestic concerns.

There is also, however, a debit side. Can Angola contain Savimbi without Cuban support? Is South Africa ready to accept the seeming certainty of a SWAPO victory in a free Namibian election? President dos Santos's sudden visit to Havana in March, his first in four years, suggests that Angola is edging toward a decision. The communiqué issued at the end of his meetings with President Fidel Castro reiterated the four conditions for a Cuban withdrawal that have been stated several times in the past: the unilateral removal of all SADF personnel from Angola, the implementation of UN Security Council Resolution 435 of 1978 setting forth procedures for Namibia's transition to independence, an end to all outside aggression against Angola, and a halt to aid for UNITA. Of these conditions, the problem of Savimbi looms largest. A reconciliation between UNITA and the MPLA (i.e. a coalition government in Luanda) would clearly be preferable. In his previously cited March 30 news conference, Savimbi offered to form a government of national unity with the Luanda regime, but warned that if his offer were rejected he would carry his guerrilla war into Angola's cities. A coalition seems unlikely, however, given the internal frailties of the MPLA and the chasm of mistrust between the MPLA and Savimbi.

An outright defeat of UNITA is an unlikely prospect in view of the movement's current military strength and strong ethnic backing among the Ovimbundu (who make up roughly 40 percent of the total population of the country) in southeastern Angola. One possibility given increasing credence is a stalemate, with the guerrilla war continuing but not on a level that directly threatens the government. According to at least one school of thought in Luanda, a UNITA deprived of South African support and with hostile black states at its rear (Zambia and a newly independent Namibia) would gradually wither away, especially if improving economic conditions strengthen popular support for the government.

Pretoria similarly appears to be moving closer to a decision. The relationship with the Angolans in the Joint Monitoring Commission, which consists of five senior officers and three companies of soldiers from each side, has encouraged the doves in the South African government and helped to mollify some of the military hawks who opposed the disengagement. The release of Herman Toivo ja Toivo, one of the founders of SWAPO, after 16 years of imprisonment on Robben Island is another straw in the wind. Press speculation that Toivo's release was a tactic to divide SWAPO by setting up a challenge to Nujoma's leadership misreads the South African mentality. In freeing Toivo, the government is acting from a position of strength; it is signaling its confidence and intentions to the other parties in the negotiating process.

The third phase of the Angolan-Namibian saga, assuming the second stage is brought to a successful conclusion, will be the implementation of the UN plan for Namibia's decolonization and independence. As envisioned by the Western Contact Group, a cease-fire in Namibia will be followed by the arrival of a multinational United Nations military force that, together with a contingent of South African police and civilians, will supervise a seven-month period of preparation culminating in the election of a constituent assembly. The task of the constituent assembly will be to write a constitution around a set of principles agreed to by South Africa and the Contact Group. Namibia will then become formally independent. During this process, Cuban troops will leave Angola as South Africa pulls its forces out of Namibia.

Although this sequence has been agreed to by all participants, some are less happy about it than others. Moreover, the Soviet Union, an interested party rather than a direct player, is clearly concerned over recent developments with regard to Angola. As military pressure from South Africa and UNITA increased in late 1983, the USSR stepped up arms shipments to Angola. In November 1983, the Soviet Union protested South Africa's regional destabilization policy in an unprecedented face-to-face meeting with South African officials at the United Nations in New

York, and underscored its position more strongly in a January 5, 1984 TASS statement that demanded an end to "direct and indirect" South African "aggression" against Angola, called for the withdrawal of South African troops from that country, and warned that "aggression cannot be left unpunished."

With the announcement of the South African-Angolan disengagement talks, these expressions of Soviet diplomatic support for Angola were given differing interpretations by Moscow and Luanda. Soviet spokesmen asserted that the November warning to Pretoria had been made at Angola's request. Angola took the position that the warning had been a Soviet initiative, and argued that in any case it had had little effect, since it was followed in just over a week by "Operation Askari," one of South Africa's largest incursions into Angola.

More recently, the Soviets, while continuing to criticize the United States and South Africa, have sought to avoid the appearance of conflict with African wishes for Namibia. An article in *Pravda* on March 5, 1984, for instance, stated that the "Soviet Union does not pursue any aims in southern Africa that would run against the aspirations of the Africans, particularly against their desire to see the Namibian question settled as soon as possible."

South Africa also has reservations about the sequence, particularly the third phase when the United Nations becomes directly involved. In Windhoek, an intensive new effort to bring together a broad coalition of the major "internal" parties is being orchestrated with Sean Cleary, assistant director of the office of the administrator-general for Namibia (and former minister in the South African Embassy in Washington), as conductor and Fanuel Kozonguizi, the first president of the South West Africa National Union (SWANU) and a former advisor to the assassinated Herero leader, Chief Clemens Kapuuo, as leader. This grouping, known as the Multi-Party Conference (MPC), includes parties ranging from the right-wing National Party through the moderate Democratic Turnhalle Alliance to SWANU and the SWAPO-Democrats. Cleary's objective is to reach a consensus on the future of the territory, especially its constitution, and then invite SWAPO to join the MPC's deliberations. If the strategy were to be successful, there would be no need for the UN to become involved. If, on the other hand, the effort to draw in SWAPO fails, there will at least be a unified and potentially powerful internal grouping to fight SWAPO in elections or whatever comes next.

It is against this background that South Africa proposed on March 11 that "all those involved in the current conflict in South West Africa/Angola," including South Africa, the Angolan government, UNITA, SWAPO, and the MPC, hold a conference to thrash out their problems. The offer was obviously a trial balloon which had little chance of flying (SWAPO and Angola rejected it immediately), but it was another reminder that Namibia's independence would be much easier for South Africa to swallow if the UN could be bypassed. The move, which took the United States by surprise, also showed that Pretoria is protective of its new role as regional superpower and (again like Israel) intends to keep as many of the cards in its hands as possible.

4. Botswana, Lesotho, Swaziland

South Africa's relation with these smaller border states, all former British trusteeship territories, have always been relatively stable and manageable. The BLS states, as they are commonly known, are even more economically dependent on South Africa than their larger black neighbors. All three are members of the Southern African Customs Union, send large numbers of migrant workers to South Africa, and depend heavily on South African ports and railways for their trade. (Indeed, Lesotho is an enclave within South Africa and relies totally on Pretoria's goodwill for access to the outside world.) The BLS regard themselves as part of the African community of nations, however, and are full members of the Organization of African Unity and the Front Line states grouping. None of the three has diplomatic relations with South Africa, although official dealings with Pretoria are commonplace and occur at the highest levels.

Swaziland has traditionally been closest to South Africa and, shortly after the signing of the Nkomati Accord, it was revealed that the Swazi and South African governments had signed a similar nonaggression pact in 1982. Discussions are currently going on between Botswana and Pretoria, and it will be no surprise if another nonaggression pact is the end product.

Lesotho is the odd man out. South Africa's relationship with the tiny, mountainous kingdom has been a bumpy one. Prime Minister (Chief) Leabua Jonathan, a tough autocrat who has ruled the country since independence in 1966, was originally seen in Pretoria as the ideal client leader: conservative, pragmatic, and pliant. For many years, Jonathan appeared to fit the bill, but in the late 1970s he adopted a much more independent line in foreign policy, including attendance at the 1979 meeting of the nonaligned states in Havana. As a result, he found himself on the receiving end of Pretoria's strong-arm tactics. These have included cross-border raids, military support for his political opponents, and temporary slowdowns of traffic across his borders. These moves brought Jonathan to heel with the result that some prominent ANC refugees have been expelled from Lesotho and an uneasy truce now exists between the two countries. South African pressure on Jonathan to join the "nonaggression club" can be expected to intensify.

Summing Up

The game is not yet over. A successful disengagement by South African and Angolan forces in southern Angola could lead to a successful parallel withdrawal of Cuban forces from Angola and South African forces from Namibia. This in turn could lead to a successful implementation of the UN plan and end with an internationally recognized independent Namibia. But that's a lot of "coulds" and much more water will have to flow under many more diplomatic bridges—including the U.S. election in November—before we will have any certainty as to the outcome. All that can be said now is that most of the players involved in the game appear to think that this is the best chance yet. They also agree that U.S. diplomacy is vital and should be given credit.

If all the pieces do indeed fall into place, there should be a lull in southern Africa, a period of adjustment and *relative* peace. The term relative is critical, because the following issues will remain unresolved:

(1) It seems unlikely that the various dissident movements—UNITA in Angola, the MNR in Mozambique, and Super-ZAPU and other groups in Zimbabwe—will reach acceptable compromises with the governments they oppose or that they will simply fade away. Destabilizing insurgencies will continue, with or without South African help.

(2) The ANC, though temporarily down, is far from out. It is being forced to rethink its strategy. Mozambique's leaders, drawing a distinction between the colonial regime formerly imposed on their own country and South Africa's status as a sovereign republic, now advise the ANC against the kind of violent military struggle waged by FRELIMO against the Portuguese prior to independence, and instead advocate concentration on nonviolent political action. Will the ANC follow the game plan proffered by Maputo? Or will it embrace something like the "Black September" strategy adopted by the PLO after its defeat in Jordan in 1970? Will the existing fissures within the ANC widen under the strain and another breakaway movement take place, as happened in 1959 when Robert Sobukwe led the young radicals out of the party to form the rival Pan-Africanist Congress?

(3) Within South Africa, the Botha government's new constitutional dispensation, granting a limited political role in the central government to the country's 2.7 million Coloureds and 850,000 Indians (Asians), has failed to address

the fundamental grievances of the 22 million blacks making up the majority of the population. Some observers are comparing the current mood among young blacks to the immediate pre-Soweto period of the mid-1970s. The South African government does not seem inclined to try to build bridges to the ANC, even though it clearly relishes its new dialogue with its black neighbors and has offered to release ANC President Nelson Mandela (who was sentenced to life imprisonment in 1964) on condition he is rusticated to the Transkei. The homeland policy, the centerpiece of grand apartheid, is enshrined in the new constitution and remains the bedrock of Pretoria's internal strategy.

(4) What happens when the Mugabes, the Machels, the dos Santoses, and the Nujomas of the Front Line states fail to meet the rapidly rising expectations of their people in the period of relative tranquility that Pax Pretoriana brings to the region?

(5) How is Moscow reassessing its options and objectives as it sees its influence reduced and replaced by that of South Africa and the United States? No dramatic moves are likely—the USSR's real priorities are elsewhere—but rather a period of watchful waiting for signs of unraveling.

If, on the other hand, the pieces of the jigsaw fail to fit into place, then the carefully wrought diplomacy could easily disintegrate. South Africa intends to maintain hegemony by talking if possible—but by more thumping if need be. Phrases such as "total onslaught" and "the Cuban threat" have faded out of the South African vocabulary to be replaced by "dialogue," "good neighborliness," and "regional cooperation," but they could quickly return if the dialogue dies out in the bush of southern Angola or along the border of Namibia.

6

Eight New Realities in Southern Africa

Heribert Adam and Stanley Uys

February 1985

1. Neocolonization

Why did South Africa suddenly modify its aggressive policy of economic and military destabilization toward its black
neighbors in 1984? Why did the heretofore implacably anti-
Pretoria socialist governments of Mozambique and Angola
suddenly agree to enter into deals with South Africa? Why
does South Africa remain Zimbabwe's principal trading
partner?

Answers commonly include the cumulative debilitating
effects of South African military and economic pressure, a
severe three-year regional drought, and the depressed world
market for most of the region's commodity exports. In the
former Portuguese territories, an additional factor was the
administrative disintegration that followed an independence
for which the colonial regime had neglected to train enough
Africans to replace the Portuguese entrepreneurial and professional intelligentsia who fled the two strife-torn countries.

The case of Mozambique is the most clear-cut. Tied to
the South African economy in manifold ways (electricity
supplies, railway and harbor connections, migrant labor re-
mittances), this exhausted neighbor decided in favor of

pragmatic survival rather than ideological martyrdom. Internal peace, accompanied by South African trade and tourists, would, it was hoped, fill the empty shops with food and the bankrupt state coffers with hard currency.

For South Africa, too, the long-term benefits of a southern African détente would be considerable:

• Formal economic hegemony is far cheaper than costly military dominance. There are clear limits to the aggressiveness that an inflation-ridden economy with severe skilled manpower problems can sustain without eroding the affluence of the ruling minority. To replace coercion with development assistance amounts to much more elegant and efficient control.

• Formalized economic collaboration with Mozambique, an independent Namibia, and Zimbabwe would reestablish the lost *cordon sanitaire*. While the strategic importance of such a buffer zone generally has been overrated, the severity of the setback for the military activity of the African National Congress (ANC) has already been demonstrated.

• The Nkomati Accord, together with the partial withdrawal of the South African Defense Force (SADF) from Angola and the establishment of a joint MPLA-South African monitoring force, cast Pretoria in the role of regional peacemaker. The renewed international legitimacy of the South African government was a much-needed ideological boost to counter growing black militancy at home.

• The economic incorporation of Front Line states into the South African orbit complicates and inhibits the drive for imposition of international economic sanctions. Insofar as the Front Line states publicly accept and extend their economic dependence on South Africa, any damage to the Republic will have a ripple effect on the clients. South Africa can justifiably argue that punitive actions against the Republic will extend to all its neighbors. In sum, the Front Line governments now have a vested interest in stalling sanctions.

• The move toward regional détente exposed the failure of socialist development economics and demonstrated the weakness of the commitment of the Soviet Union and its allies to the region. This "de-Marxification" will not be lost on black opinion inside South Africa. Pragmatic stances rather than ideological postures are determining economic policies and external links throughout the area.

• The rapprochement is a setback for the Southern African Development Coordination Conference (SADCC). Set up in 1980 by nine southern African black governments and assisted by Western aid, its declared purpose is to lessen the dependence of the member states' economies on the Republic. SADCC represents an economic response to a political problem, whereas only a political reconciliation can resolve the economic disparity. The Nkomati Accord amounts to a recognition of this contradiction, ratifying the reality of increased rather than lessening incorporation of the Front Line economies into the South African orbit. Zimbabwe's trade with its SADCC partners, for example, has fallen since the organization's inception in 1980, and the goal of pruning long-established economic linkages with the South African powerhouse for political reasons was doomed from the start. The dependence of the Front Line states on South African transport links has been increased by the continuing turmoil within Mozambique. Indeed, SADCC, at this stage, would benefit from South African membership – provided no political strings were attached.

In shifting from destabilization to détente, Pretoria banked on the assumption that the governments of Mozambique and Angola would give higher priority to staying in power than to their loathing of apartheid. Faced with the options of steady collapse or pragmatic capitulation to save the core, both the FRELIMO government in Maputo and the MPLA in Luanda chose survival.

Despite the public pronouncements of friendship, the South African government's position is one of paternalistic arrogance toward its neighbors, whose economic and political failings are seen as demonstrating not only the superiority of capitalism but, more important for domestic consumption, the chaotic consequences of majority rule. As even a relatively well-endowed country such as Zimbabwe slides into a pattern of repressing minorities and violating civil rights, the appeal within South Africa of the liberal-socialist alternative is significantly tarnished.

2. Mozambique: A New Ideological Mix

Mozambique's signature of the Nkomati Accord proved correct Marx's assumption that true socialism cannot be built on hungry stomachs. Administrative disintegration overwhelmed a postindependence effort at ideological mobilization that failed to engage the country's vast hinterland. Even with its sizable South African support, the campaign of guerrilla warfare by the MNR would have had far less impact without the apathy of large sections of Mozambique's rural poor toward FRELIMO.

This state of affairs has reduced the FRELIMO and many other African versions of freedom ideology to a rhetorical socialism in which the slogans bandied by the urban elite fail to stir the underprivileged peasants. The rhetoric placates Eastern bloc sponsors and creates a progressive image abroad but is hardly taken seriously even by its own proponents. In a crunch, the elite will readily modify ideological interpretations to meet the needs of the occasion, since it has little collective commitment to the existing ideology. This opportunistic socialism is accepting practical capitalist techniques under a new formula that turns defeat into victory. Instead of explaining the national predicament to the people, Mozambican propaganda presented the Nkomati Accord as a heroic victory over South Africa. The irony of a smiling Machel, the victim, in a London-tailored marshal's uniform and a dour P.W. Botha, the destabilizer, in a rumpled civilian suit could hardly have been lost on a more sophisticated television audience. Each side could believe it had upstaged the other.

The FRELIMO leadership need not fear an ideological rebellion against its change of course as long as it can deliver the new goods. With government-controlled media, the leadership can manipulate domestic opinion to a great degree and need only be concerned with practical success. This means FRELIMO cannot be halfhearted about its adherence to the treaty, as the ANC had hoped, since FRELIMO's own fate is bound up with Nkomati's success. Therefore, Mozambique and the other "socialist" clients of South Africa now have a vested interest in economic stability and evolutionary rather than revolutionary change in the Republic. Under these circumstances, the ANC is perceived as a threat to progress and development in neighboring states.

As they become locked into increased economic ties with South Africa, the Front Line states become more dependent on the bond and will be increasingly unable to cut it at will. The policy of détente, therefore, is not just a tactical retreat that can ultimately be repudiated. Nor will Mozambique or the others be able to "use capitalism against itself." As the dependent and weaker party, Maputo is not in a position to dictate the terms for business involvement.

Yet it would be wrong to perceive the Front Line states as having become Bantustans. They are not South African creations but sovereign entities whose populations, unlike those of the Bantustans, identify with the political leadership. Their greater maneuverability, therefore, cannot be compared with the total dependence on Pretoria of the Matanzimas and Sebes.

This is why an overthrow of FRELIMO was not and is not in Pretoria's interest. Likewise, it is wrong to assume that South Africa would benefit from replacing (if it were possible) the MPLA in Luanda with a UNITA regime. Were either of these events to occur, South Africa would have to prop up another unpopular government, and dealing with several "Namibias" at once is something beyond Pretoria's financial and military capabilities. It is far preferable to pluck the fruits of economic hegemony without taking on new administrative responsibilities.

Whether the benefits of closer economic ties with South Africa will in fact materialize remains uncertain. If South Africa is unable to turn its own homelands into showpieces, it is unlikely to turn a much larger Mozambique into a success story. While Pretoria has signed some trade agreements and South Africans have channeled some funds into tourism, agriculture, fishing, and harbor development, the personnel and resources are lacking to undertake a massive development program in a high-risk country like Mozambique. Even if South Africa accepts many more Mozambican mine workers, redirects freight through Maputo, and buys more electricity from the Cabora Bassa complex, this will only marginally help to alleviate Mozambique's poverty. For the foreseeable future, Mozambique will continue to rely on foreign aid, particularly from the Scandinavian countries. As a charity case and client state, its political dependency on the new donors will increase as long as its East European patrons are unwilling to pick up the tab.

3. From "Liberation" to "Civil Rights"

In the process of justifying the Nkomati Accord to the Mozambican people, FRELIMO has made a fundamental shift in its public stand on the domestic situation in South Africa. Maputo has redefined the conflict within South Africa as "a civil rights struggle," implicitly abandoning the revolutionary hope in favor of reformist expectations. Suggesting that black civil rights can be achieved without altering the structure of domination implicitly accepts the notion that blacks could be incorporated into a nonracial capitalism — an idea that flies in the face of the Marxist assumption that apartheid and capitalism are inseparable in South Africa.

The now-jettisoned notion of "liberation" had been based on the idea that South Africa is a *colonial* entity controlled by a minority *settler* regime. Machel has now made explicit reference to the *anticolonial* struggles of the Afrikaners in the Boer War and has referred to Afrikaners as *Africans*. These comments by an African leader with impeccable anticolonial and socialist credentials constitute an unprecedented legitimation of the Republic. While the Lusaka Manifesto of April 1969 had offered South Africa similar legitimacy on the condition that Pretoria abandon apartheid, the Machel recognition came without conditions attached. The Mozambican stance does not imply approval of or indifference toward apartheid. Instead, it signals a recognition that Maputo is in no position to force change on Pretoria and that a major internal restructuring in South Africa is unlikely in the foreseeable future.

Mozambique is not the only Front Line state moving toward disengagement from the apartheid issue. Angola's President José Eduardo dos Santos stated in an interview published in *The Washington Post* on October 14, 1984 that he is prepared to live "in an atmosphere of tolerance" with South Africa once Namibia is independent. Apartheid and white minority rule should be condemned by all nations, dos Santos said, but he suggested that they would be treated as internal problems when South Africa, "which is very far away from Angola," returns to its borders. This served as one more reminder to South African blacks that, Organization of African Unity rhetoric notwithstanding, they are on their own. The rising incidence of township unrest may be a sign that black South Africans have finally grasped this message.

4. There Is No "Master Plan"

Pretoria's regional policy-making apparatus is neither monolithic nor as streamlined as the "scientific management charts" introduced since Botha's ascendancy suggest. The academic debates about the role of the military and the State Security Council obscure the simple fact that there is no master plan for southern Africa. Interbureaucratic rivalries and personality idiosyncrasies influence decisions, as do career and status considerations of the few dozen persons involved. Only a few senior military officers support the efforts of a Department of Foreign Affairs sensitive to international opinion to reach a neocolonial disengagement in Angola and Mozambique and an internationally acceptable settlement in Namibia. The Department of Military Intelligence (DMI), unlike the less influential National Intelligence Service (NIS), views the present version of détente as premature. The police leadership, on the other hand, supports the Nkomati Accord because of its impact on the ANC.

All this is in marked contrast to the usual Western perception of the upper military echelons as enlightened technocrats and the police as heavy-handed traditionalists. While the role of the South African military in the administrative disunity of the government is similar to that of its counterparts elsewhere, there is one significant difference: the virtual veto power inherent in the informal influence of a half-dozen senior officers who cling to the belief that South Africa's "enemies" can more reliably be subdued by covert and open force than by political incorporation.

This diversity of opinion in Pretoria enables the United States to exercise more informal influence over South Africa's policies than it would if there were a monolithic decision-making process. On the other hand, the Reagan administration's "constructive engagement" is not nearly as influential as its supporters and critics claim. It was not international pressure, but rather the clear weakness of the Republic's right-wing ideologues evidenced in the outcome of the November 1983 constitutional referendum, that gave the ruling technocrats the confidence to shift from military destabilization to a pragmatic policy of neocolonization. It would be political suicide for any Afrikaner politician to be perceived as "in the Americans' pocket." The insistence on homespun solutions is more than just a means of garnering votes through anti-Americanism. Unlike white Americans in the 1960s, South African whites cannot expect to keep political control if the country moves to a universal franchise.

Generally speaking, there are in 1985 three schools of thought in Pretoria concerning an Angolan-Namibian settlement: (1) one school (which includes much of the SADF leadership) is opposed to any Namibian settlement that would lead to SWAPO taking over in Windhoek; (2) another school, which includes some SADF elements and some politicians, would accept a settlement if the terms were right; (3) a third school, for reasons including cost and international legitimacy, has adopted a positive attitude toward a settlement and is pushing for one. President P.W. Botha and Minister of Foreign Affairs Roelof ("Pik") Botha are believed to be prepared to see SWAPO eventually become the majority party, because they are confident that Namibia's economic interdependence with South Africa will keep it in orbit.

South African policy on Namibia must take account of certain physical constraints. Unlike Mozambique, Angola is too distant and too heavily supported to be throttled easily. Lacking a common border with South Africa, Angola need not become economically beholden to the Republic. Moreover, the SADF's 1960s-vintage aircraft would be a poor match against Angola's Soviet-supplied MiG-23s and Mi-24 helicopter gunships should fighting escalate. During the SADF's late 1983 "Operation Askari," the South Africans were surprised by the resistance they encountered from Angolan forces and by the sophistication of the Soviet weaponry. Moreover, the Soviet Union has invested sufficient support and prestige in Angola that it might feel compelled to respond to a heightened South African threat to the MPLA with an escalation of its own involvement. The question also arises as to whether Pretoria could simultaneously cope with widespread unrest in South Africa's black townships and wage a neocolonial war in Angola. Even at its present intensity, the war on "the border" is not popular among South Africa's whites, although most of the opposition is muted.

In 1984, Pretoria played for a while with the idea of separating the Angolan-Cuban question from that of a Namibian settlement. Despite its stated adherence to UN Security Council Resolution 435, Pretoria has sought to circumvent a UN role in supervising a disengagement of troops and free elections in the territory. If the Angolan-South African joint monitoring force could control SWAPO's military activity, then the need for a UN military presence would arguably have disappeared, especially if SWAPO were to shift from military to political activity in anticipation of Namibian independence. The transition to independence could then be legitimized through Front Line acceptance and perhaps token military participation rather than through the UN plan, and Pretoria's hand would be correspondingly strengthened.

Paradoxically, this regional scenario would also have phased out the U.S. broker role. South Africa would have benefited from being seen as having initiated Namibian independence. Pretoria's apparent control of events would have dampened the elation of South Africa's blacks over the emergence of another independent black state on their doorstep.

As of early 1985, however, Pretoria seems to hope that Angola can be pressured (partly through UNITA) to force SWAPO into a cease-fire and into a provisional "government of national unity" in Namibia. The ongoing township unrest inside South Africa has also contributed to a renewed reluctance on the part of the government to be seen as handing over Namibia to a guerrilla liberation movement. On the other hand, South Africa's deepening fiscal crisis makes it ever more imperative to shed the costly burden of maintaining militarily a large and largely useless colony when the resources are urgently needed at home.

According to R.H. Green of the Institute of Development Studies at Sussex University, as much as 9 percent of total South African government expenditure is for Namibia. Green calculates the true figure to be almost twice that of the officially reported R1.143 billion. By the end of 1984, the territory's foreign debt was around R700 million, with gross borrowing of R200 million, suggesting a debt service of R175 million – 20 percent of its export earnings and over a quarter of its probable local revenue for 1985. With a declining agricultural output since 1977, a ruined fishing industry, and a stagnating mining sector, only uranium mining by Rio Tinto Zinc's Rössing group continues to be profitable. In this situation, any independent Namibian government, regardless of ideological outlook, will start with a heavy dependency on the regional superpower.

5. Changing Trade-Offs with the West

The historic Botha tour of Western Europe in May and June 1984 has been variously portrayed as a breakthrough in South Africa's diplomatic isolation; as a reward for Nkomati, the abandonment of destabilization policies, and concessions on Namibian independence; and as an attempt to gain international legitimacy for Pretoria's constitutional reforms. All this misses the main purpose of South Africa's diplomatic quest. Pretoria alone cannot foot the bill for a successful neocolonization of southern Africa. In Botha's own words, the government is not in a position to play Father Christmas.

To maintain domestic stability, it must focus on job creation in South Africa's own impoverished hinterland. The development capital of R1.5 billion which the Republic has guaranteed to its own "Development Bank of Southern Africa" exhausts Pretoria's financial capabilities, which have been hit hard by recessionary trends and a depressed gold price. In short, serious domestic employment creation and external development aid preclude each other.

On the other hand, South Africa would be the main beneficiary of an extended regional common market. Given the underdeveloped purchasing power of the domestic market, South African capital can utilize economies of scale only if it has access to outlets abroad. Ever since Prime Minister Vorster's short-lived outward policy in the late 1960s, the main thrust of the developing government and private sector alliance has been to overcome the political barriers to the underdeveloped markets of black Africa. Despite the international rhetoric of isolation and boycotts, South African firms have gradually succeeded in gaining access throughout most of independent Africa, albeit usually on a clandestine basis.

The major impediments to accelerated private sector expansion in the southern region are (1) the lack of infrastructure and security in countries such as Mozambique and (2) political uncertainty, particularly in Namibia and Angola. Private investment needs both long-term commitments and predictability of risks. Therefore, it depends heavily on the role of Western development aid and international legitimacy in creating stable trade and investment conditions. If, for example, West Germany were to adopt Namibia as a client in the same way that it rescued a bankrupt Turkey for the Western alliance, or that France looks after its former African territories, South Africa's costs would be reduced and the Republic would also indirectly benefit from such development aid. The same would apply if the United States and Britain were to channel significant support to Mozambique.

The concept of neocolonial cooperation between South Africa and the West obviously faces obstacles. Visible contact with the white minority regime remains a sensitive issue in Europe and the United States. Even the West's conservatives are now increasingly critical of apartheid, as racist "kith-and-kin" sentiment takes a back seat to a new vision of exporting free enterprise to the Third World. To those who yearn to confront socialist systems with a superior capitalist performance, South Africa is an embarrassing ally that allows only a few of its own blacks to make a profit according to market principles. The cool receptions and public condemnations of apartheid by Botha's skeptical hosts in Europe reflect a reluctance to spend freely to underwrite Pretoria's development role; they would prefer to see South Africa acting as their regional agent without their having to assume major financial responsibilities. South Africans, who are given to exaggerating their country's importance, often forget that they compete with other more attractive areas for the global cash flow.

It remains an open question whether and how Western governments will utilize the political leverage flowing from South Africa's new interest in their regional involvement. Could a trade-off emerge between concessions on apartheid and increased Western financing of southern African common market projects? Certainly, a return to repression and hard-line policies by Pretoria would strengthen support for boycotts and continued isolation. Conversely, any reformist trends inside South Africa would be welcomed by powerful outside forces in the public and private sector that are as yet wary of the risks of dealing openly with a racist state.

Beyond the politics of imagery there is also the lingering fear that any widespread unrest inside South Africa could spill over into client states and affect the growth potential of the entire region. The price for Western economic participation in the region will depend to a great extent on the muscle of the various political lobbies in Western capitals. The minimum in the way of required concrete reform will certainly exceed Sullivan-type codes, and will involve more credible forms of black political participation as well as some further symbolic legislative reforms. In particular, the unexpected surge of the boycott lobby in the United States in recent months may eventually make continued U.S. investment in South Africa conditional on a phaseout of influx control and the migratory labor system, with increased provision of housing near the workplace. Together with massive investment in black education and meaningful black political participation, these steps could be cited by the U.S. government as proof of the questioned success potential of "constructive engagement."

6. The Decline of "Total Onslaught"

As noted above, the ANC feels "betrayed" by the Front Line states. Not only was the ANC not consulted during the Nkomati negotiations, but the conditions of the movement's future operation (and expulsion) from Mozambique proved rather "uncomradely," as one observer put it. The continued "moral, political, and diplomatic support" of the ANC promised by Mozambique is restricted to a 10-member diplomatic office for which names had to be submitted for approval (six were rejected).

In Zimbabwe, Prime Minister Robert Mugabe denies the ANC training facilities not only because of fear of South African reprisals but also because the Moscow-linked ANC supported his rival, Joshua Nkomo, during the country's war of independence. Angolan-South African military cooperation bodes ill for the ANC training camps in Angola. ANC members have been expelled or pressured to depart from Swaziland and Lesotho. All this leaves distant Tanzania and Zambia, which are Front Line states in name only.

These setbacks are not sufficient to destroy the ANC, but they may well force a cutback in the organization's sabotage activities and cause it to rethink its military strategy. A more politically minded ANC, using unions and other above-ground organizations, may concentrate on areas where apartheid's defenses are weakest and its opponents strongest.

While the occasional ANC incursions from Mozambique were never viewed as a serious threat by Pretoria's inner circles, the government found it useful to exaggerate the ANC threat (and the Cuban presence in Angola) to mobilize white support against a Soviet-orchestrated "total onslaught." "Adapt or die" admonitions are credible only if the dying is a demonstrated alternative, not merely a vague prophecy. When government leaders now plead for consensus, inveigh against confrontation, and warn of the costs of revolutionary turmoil, they repeat a theme which has for decades been the basis of liberal opposition to apartheid. But by co-opting the cry of doom, the government implies that it has the foresight to avert disaster. It can lead the way out of the pending apocalypse if it has the unquestioned support for racial reforms of a racist constituency.

Thus, the peace pact with Mozambique undermined one of the key justifications for the disputed reforms – the threat from an all-pervasive outside enemy. It rendered obsolete the ideology of the "total onslaught" and similar myths like "the border," manufactured to rally support for domestic militarization. Communism is still being peddled as a unifying menace, but this claim is becoming increasingly difficult to sustain.

The Soviet Union remains the major arms supplier for the ANC and SWAPO, but has not acquired naval or military bases anywhere in the region, despite treaties of friendship and cooperation with Angola and Mozambique. Indeed, it is much more prudent for Moscow to let South Africa fester as the obvious racial sore of capitalism than to seek an escalating confrontation with the West in this distant arena. For all these reasons, South Africa ranks low in terms of Moscow's global priorities.

It is noteworthy that, despite its concern about Soviet expansionism, the Reagan administration does not share the common South African perception of the Soviet Union as being intent to lay its hands on the subcontinent's treasures. In a November 1983 speech in Munich, for example, U.S. Deputy Assistant Secretary for African Affairs Frank Wisner observed: "Southern Africa is, practically speaking, well outside the Soviet Union's zone of primary interest, indeed of its secondary interests. We believe that Moscow is aware of that fact and, in reality, spends little time thinking about the area."

7. Changes in Anti-Apartheid Politics

If sanctions against South Africa are no longer in the interest of some Front Line states which themselves are now participating in ending the isolation of the apartheid state, then the international antiapartheid movement will also have to rethink its politics. The likely outcome in the long run is a split between those committed to military confrontation and those willing to participate in internal reform. What shape such a division will take depends on what channels of legitimate political participation are open to radical apartheid opponents.

South Africa's new tricameral parliamentary system does not represent a step toward the inclusion of blacks in the political process. The racist logic of the 1984 constitution does not lend itself to the kind of adaptation that would allow a legalized ANC to participate without committing political suicide. Even if the government were to release Nelson Mandela (a likely development), welcome back exiles committed to peace, and offer to consult with the ANC and its United Democratic Front allies about a new deal, there is not much to negotiate about unless the agenda involves scrapping the constitution and starting over again. Despite all the admonitions about an internal peace accord, the government remains at a loss about how to accommodate black demands for direct and meaningful political participation in central decision making.

This impasse forces political activists to work clandestinely in legal bodies and to politicize unions, churches, and student groups. While authorities thus may succeed in prying away individuals from specific resistance movements, the same people are then also no longer bound by organizational discipline. Such fragmentation of an opponent may be celebrated as a victory by the power-holders, but it can backfire. It takes only a few atomized and alienated individuals to cause havoc in an industrial society, as the terrorism of fringe groups in the capitals of the world proves almost daily.

Despite the car bombs in South African cities, the ANC leadership, including the Communist Party element, has so far successfully resisted pressure to resort to "terrorist" activities, i.e. the deliberate killing of white civilians. This has recently been reiterated by the ANC's president, Oliver

Tambo, and its secretary-general, Alfred Nzo. But a deepening gap between the exiled ANC leadership and internal militants who are no longer under the control of a tight authoritarian organization might well prove to be a Pyrrhic victory for the government. The strategic planners in the State Security Council may yet regret having achieved the weakening of a movement of great symbolic value for the mass of victims, and may grow nostalgic for the day when they could pinpoint a politically predictable and reliable opponent for negotiations instead of having to deal with unmanageable anarchy.

Such difficulties do not arise in negotiations between states. It is easier for two hostile but sovereign states to reach an accord than for diverse domestic parties to do the same. The question for South Africa remains: how can the pending peaceful coexistence between the states of the region be extended to South Africa's more fundamental internal conflicts? A unified, cohesive movement that could legitimately represent and bargain for the underdog may indeed be in the interest of those most fearful about their security. On the other hand, the likely pluralism of black opposition groups with different ideologies and interests could also strengthen the chances of a democratic system.

8. The Logic of an ANC-Afrikaner "Indaba"

Lasting stability in South Africa now depends more than ever on negotiations between Afrikaners of the National Party and what are usually referred to as "the authentic leaders of the black masses." There is little doubt that, among the many black leaders with a following, the outlawed ANC, with its hidden constituency in the UDF, ranks top among politicized urban blacks, although it is by no means the sole representative of black opinion.

With a remarkable insensitivity to the rejection of collaborating blacks by the more politicized segments they are supposed to control, the government officially emphasizes their leadership role while publicly ignoring the real representatives. This only enhances the credibility of the rejected. Thus, any public hint that a given black has engaged in consultations with the government now amounts to a kiss of death. Even the exiled ANC president would immediately be suspected of selling out a militant internal leadership if he were to fly to Pretoria tomorrow. Hence, both sides have a vital interest in keeping contacts secret for different reasons: black activists cannot afford to be compromised, while the government does not want to be seen as weak by its electorate because it is negotiating with an official enemy.

What are the prospects for serious talks beyond the informal individual contacts and proxy dialogues already taking place? The positive results of Pretoria's 1981–1983 strategy of aggressive regional destabilization and the general militarization of the country have encouraged the voices that advocate resorting to traditional coercion. On the other side, there is a growing realization that the township unrest may be containable militarily but can only be solved politically. Individual white business leaders such as Tony Bloom have urged the government to realize the "historic inevitability" of talks with the ANC. In December 1984, under the impact of successful strike action, organized business spoke out forcefully for the first time against traditional repression of union leadership, on whom it increasingly depends for industrial peace.

Although the Afrikaner business segment soon retracted its statements after a meeting with Minister of Law and Order Louis le Grange, the influence of business on government is likely to increase. With a worsening economic crisis, the massive costs generated by apartheid will become the obvious target for savings. In forums ranging from a cabinet committee to the Urban Foundation of big business and the Human Sciences Research Council of academia, dozens of eager attempts have been made to formulate possible "solutions to intergroup relations." Their common thread lies in a "management approach" that implies continued white control with sufficient modifications to appease, contain, manipulate, and co-opt black militancy. Only a minority of these proposals provide for an open-ended dialogue, and even fewer advocate serious negotiations about formulas of power sharing that would be mutually agreed upon instead of imposed.

Nevertheless, ever since Ton Vosloo, then the editor of *Beeld*, became in 1980 the first prominent Nationalist to suggest that the government eventually would have to negotiate with the ANC, this proposition has gained wider currency among technocratic power-holders. It is speculated, for example, that the purchase of the semiweekly *City Press* by Vosloo's Nasionale Pers group in 1984 was motivated in part by a desire to provide the National Party with a credible outlet in the black newspaper market by which such a dialogue could be carried out and influenced. Voices that express willingness to negotiate range from President Botha to Afrikaner journalists and Pretoria's ambassador to London, "provided it is done peacefully and not under the threat of violence."

Both sides have stated their formal bargaining positions: Botha wants the ANC to renounce violence, and the ANC wants Botha to abandon apartheid. Within the broad interpretations of these terms there may well be significant areas of common interest and possible compromise: federalism, regional economic development, decentralization of power to nonracial local authorities, and citizenship regulations for newly defined larger homeland areas. The crucial test will be to what extent Pretoria is prepared to abandon the imposed racial ordering of South African society in favor of voluntary group associations.

The flurry of statements regarding Pretoria-ANC negotiations are part of a Western-supported campaign to follow up on the Mozambican reorientation by also drawing the ANC into closer alignment with the West. Success here would make life far more difficult for Pretoria's hard-liners than if the ANC were to remain safely labeled "Communist." Nonetheless, it would obviously suit South Africa if the

ANC were to suspend its military activity as part of a formal summit.

While the summit is a distant possibility, a truce is not. On the government's part, there is no intention whatsoever at this time of offering the ANC a share in political decision making. By showing willingness to talk, Pretoria hopes to exploit differences within the ANC and eventually split the organization into so-called radical Communists and compromising "nationalists." Pretoria's first choice is obviously not to incorporate them as a partner in power.

Meanwhile, the pressures on the ANC to place armed struggle on hold in favor of political dialogue are not confined to the likelihood that further military action in South Africa would be futile and might ultimately lead to cynical demoralization among the organization's adherents when the promised liberation failed to materialize. Beyond this, Front Line leaders, especially Machel and Zambia's President Kenneth Kaunda, are leaning on the organization to fall in line with their own designs.

In the past, such Front Line persuasion has often had a decisive effect on specific stances of liberation movements, even if the guests perceived their interests differently from their hosts. But the recent distancing between the Front Line states and the ANC, together with the attempt to shift more responsibility for the ANC to an inefficient OAU, will lead to a decline of Front Line influence on the ANC. Already, for example, the ANC leadership in Lusaka prefers to have direct contacts with National Party representatives rather than deal with them through the good offices of its host, as was the procedure for the first official SWAPO-Pretoria encounter.

There is also an occasional reported hesitancy among trained cadres in the field to be used as cannon fodder. Those students joining the battle fresh from South Africa often are more militant than those who have undergone lengthy periods of preparation abroad. Moreover, as noted earlier, there is a potential division within the organization between those who favor an escalation of military action against "soft" targets, regardless of the casualties involved, and those who merely want to use the occasional bomb as a reminder to Pretoria to start negotiating.

This split does not necessarily coincide with the often-perceived division between alleged militant Marxists and moderate nationalists. Those with allegiance to the Communist Party tend to have a greater concern for organizational public relations and the international ramifications of a "terrorist image" than those with a less articulated ideological commitment. Last but not least, relics of the Christian tradition of nonviolence and Gandhian pacifism still linger among sections of the ANC leadership steeped deeply in the nonviolent resistance campaign of earlier decades.

While the Communist ideologues within the ANC have a lengthy timetable for the structural transformation of the adversary, most of the leadership is concerned about forestalling premature action. With vital connections to the operational zone cut by the Nkomati Accord, the guerrillas operating inside South Africa are now more difficult to control and to discipline. Indeed, the ANC has already found it necessary to issue public apologies for embarrassing mistakes made by its militant cadres. In addition to the image problem generated by such incidents, there is also real concern about the possibility that an escalation of sabotage would be met by more brutal repression.

Above all, the exiled ANC leadership faces a growing competition from a new generation of internal militants. Out of the country for 20 years, the "veterans of the struggle" are pressed to make a choice as to how long the "waiting for liberation" should last. Faced with a union movement reluctant to subject itself to the organizational discipline of populist political leadership, the ANC has to assert its symbolic role as the oldest resistance movement. Most of the union officials now have a vested interest in their own workers' organizations as against a party political organization. If a power conflict were to arise between the internal and external wings, the former would be more likely to prevail, inasmuch as the internal activists are today more steeped in the reality of struggle.

For all these reasons, the external ANC leadership must show interest in the idea of a national convention. Such a convention would mean recognition by the adversary of the ANC's legitimate role. It would give the exiled faction a platform to assert its hegemony over internal competitors, particularly independent unions and Chief Buthelezi's Inkatha movement. However, it is difficult to envisage what role the ANC (banned as a political organization in South Africa since 1960) could play as an *identifiable* organization if it is demilitarized, as South Africa demands as a precondition for talks.

The national convention option – even if the convention is perceived as an ongoing process rather than a onetime summit – is further complicated by the existence of substantial opposition groups that do not subscribe to ANC or UDF strategies. Inkatha in particular stands out as a force with organizational clout that could be a key factor in any concerted action. Despite mutual hostility in the wake of the 1979 failure of talks in London between Inkatha and the ANC, there is still less antagonism toward Buthelezi among the ANC leadership abroad than among UDF activists in the Transvaal. Unlike the UDF leadership, which rejected an alliance with Inkatha in the constitutional struggle, some exiles are prepared to accept Buthelezi (but not the Matanzimas and Sebes) at the conference table. In their view, Buthelezi is too shrewd a tactician not to side with the emerging new power group. Buthelezi, on the other hand, is not about to let himself be absorbed by the ANC.

In the unlikely event that an ANC faction succeeds in persuading the United Nations to declare the organization the sole representative of the disenfranchised South African people, the rupture with competing antiapartheid groups would become permanent. But if the broad spectrum of internal interests can assert itself in a populist "Congress" movement, the present ANC itself might change. There is no sociological law that imposes the authoritarian characteristics and moral conduct of an opponent on those striving to displace that opponent. If the future organized resistance in South Africa can institutionalize authentic grass-roots influence, as many unions have done, rather than allowing itself to be manipulated from above by all kinds of external interests, then not only a free and democratic movement but also a much more powerful opponent to apartheid will have emerged.

7

Seven Scenarios for South Africa

Robert I. Rotberg

October 1985

South Africa has seven possible destinies. From left to right the seven rubrics are: (1) Revolution, (2) Substantial Regime Change, (3) Power Sharing, (4) Limited Power Sharing, (5) Concessions, (6) Change But No Change, and (7) Reaction and Retrenchment.

The least likely scenarios – those hardest to imagine being realized – are the two extreme ones at either end of the continuum. This is a testimony to the extent to which South Africa has evolved politically. No matter how virulent and enduring the unrest of 1985, the country's ruling cadre has clearly undergone a profound shift in outlook since the days of Prime Minister Vorster. South Africa is no longer a country where whites believe that apartheid as a political program can ensure the continued dominance of whites over blacks. Likewise, Africans no longer accept their subjugation or believe that whites can magically make the power of black numbers disappear. A process of evolution has begun and is accelerating. The violence and repression of 1984–1985 have hastened the pace of change objectively and, also in terms of both white and black thinking. Political participation has emerged as the only sure bridge across the abyss dividing black and white aspirations for this beautiful, rich, and potentially powerful country.

Reaction and Retrenchment (7)

For all of these reasons, Reaction and Retrenchment (Scenario 7) has the least analytical power of all of the scenarios. It presupposes the coming of the Conservative and Herstigte Nasionale parties to power (on the lines of the National Party takeover of 1948) following a major lurch to the right as a result of adverse white reaction to reform initiatives of the present government. Theoretically, the general election results of 1989 could produce such a reversal. Or events before 1989 could lead to a military coup or a massive defection of sitting members of the National Party away from their government. But there are profound historical as well as psychological reasons for doubting whether such a shift would or could take place, particularly in the charged atmosphere that is the reality of South Africa now and for the near future.

But there is a second point. Scenario 7 presupposes a turning back of the clock, a withdrawal of present overtures to the world and to Africans, as insufficient and as unsatisfactory as those overtures may be. This is a laager scenario, but South Africa has never known political laagers. Its leaders, even in the darkest of days, have always known how to retreat. They have known how to reach the exits, how to reformulate their positions, and how to find the high ground of flexibility. Even a regime farther to the political right than the present one would, willy-nilly, find itself somewhere within Scenario 6 – Change But No Change. The path of evolution is one which permits deviations, but no total turnabouts. To walk more slowly, or even to walk in place, is possible, but this could be a feature of Scenario 6, not 7.

Revolution (1)

At the opposite end of the spectrum is Scenario 1, Revolution. Revolutions, in the classical sense, occur when the state loses legitimacy – when it can no longer impose its authority. When the state can no longer compel obedience, then the regime is overthrown, or it weakens, decays, and is pushed aside. The breakdown begins when the lower orders become disaffected, perceive the power of the state to be past, and follow new leaders and new ideologies.

Since the state relies on a military institution to assert itself, and since the noncommissioned ranks of armies and police forces are by definition composed of lower orders or at least representatives of the lower orders, the disaffection of that section of a state's citizenry automatically signals the collapse of the state. In Iran, for example, the Ayatollah Khomeini's message commanded the attention of more and more members of Iran's military rank and file. When those lower orders perceived the likely victory of the mullahs, dissatisfaction with the Shah was transformed into disaffiliation, and the revolution began.

It is immensely difficult to devise a theoretical framework for a South African revolution. The popular employment of that label is unhelpful, for a revolution is a total destruction of the prevailing order, not simply a shift in the composition of the ruling class (Scenario 2). In the case of South Africa, the potential revolutionaries may possess sufficient grievances, but they lack funds, arms, materiel, and the other standard building blocks of a late twentieth-century revolution.

It is arguable that those components might in future be more readily available than at present. Moreover, sanctuaries and outside supporters—so crucial in the North Vietnamese and the Chinese successes—may become more available despite the current hegemony of South Africa in its neighborhood. On the other hand, there are some analytical and practical reasons why sanctuaries are likely to remain unavailable and revolution as a total concept unrealizable.

The military forces of South Africa may be 6 to 10 percent nonwhite, and those percentages may increase. But the lower ranks of South Africa's standing and conscript armies, as well as the numerous reserves ("Commandos"), will in this century remain overwhelmingly white. If the struggle for South Africa is between white and black, and not between different classes or different ideological persuasions, then no revolution fueled by a shift in the allegiance of the army will occur so long as the state continues to recruit its soldiers from among the ranks of those whose very way of life is at stake. Unlike the case in Portugal in 1974, the soldiers (as well as officers) of the South African Defense Force have no obvious self-interest in refusing to shoulder arms in defense of the present state.

Change But No Change (6)

Scenario 6 describes South Africa in 1985. Africans protest violently in recurring cycles which have varying amplitudes but which ebb and flow across the geographical face of South Africa. The state may have difficulty restoring peace and tranquility, but its ultimate authority is mortgaged in no overwhelming sense. That is, ordinary police tactics of crowd control are barely sufficient to impose law and order, but the firepower of the army is held largely in reserve. Indeed, although it is analytically likely that the repressive force of the state fuels much of the rioting (goading participants to challenge police patrols and so on) and that many of the townships are today ungovernable, it does not necessarily follow that this year's violence begets greater violence, and then even more violence, and that the state crumbles. Recurrent and intensified violence is certain in South Africa, but neither its intensification nor its effects will necessarily be governed by lineal rules of progression.

Within the framework of Scenario 6, the state combines repression with the granting of concessions. Furthermore, the concessions follow limited consultation between the state and representatives of the protesters. In order to contain the riots, to stabilize the townships, to appease the West, to buy time, and so on, the state is prepared to improve the conditions under which Africans live, work, and play. The state and the white political system thus offer changes—smoothings of the evolutionary path—which whites and the state believe are significant. That is, they constitute major alterations in the ways in which whites were for so long led to believe that their relations with Africans should be arranged, as well as in the place of Africans within the overall structure of South African society. Yet whatever assertions the state makes about the significance of its concessions, Africans regard "concessions" as cosmetic or irrelevant or both, whatever their nature and objective validity.

The state, within the confines of Scenario 6, is prepared to continue or even to accelerate its program of reform while asserting the importance of a top-down orchestration of the reform process. Africans, however, no longer want to be on the receiving end of reform. They demand participation in the process itself—in the negotiation of reforms that will be meaningful. Naturally the state—any state—finding itself in this scenario knows that to negotiate the nature of change means a derogation of the authority of the state, and a weakening of its sinews of war.

Likewise, it is fundamental to Scenario 6 that protesters and their leaders believe that they will lose the momentum of their protest if they accept concessions as improvements decided upon unilaterally. In addition to such tactical considerations, the disaffected majority in South Africa has decidedly moved beyond a willingness to receive proffered economic and social benefits to an awareness that their political weaknesses can only be rectified by an insistence upon political participation. Thus, although the state wants to reform meaningfully (but more slowly than Africans desire), the state is not yet willing to accept the basic elements of the prevailing black demand for political participation and for *negotiating* its translation into practical policies.

This scenario—an abbreviated, abstracted description of the present dilemma—is important for what follows in the scenario-building exercise. It describes state immobility masquerading as forward movement. The state offers

what it considers to be meaningful change. Blacks reject
that change. And since blacks reject it, the label of Change
But No Change is apt. Yet the levels of rhetoric are high in
this phase: the state attempts to persuade its own supporters, Africans, and foreigners that its intentions are
good but that it needs time. It talks about threats from the
right (which may not be false). It hints, it frets, and there is
some lack of cohesion within the ruling party. But in this
phase either leadership or resolution is lacking for the kinds
of strategic repositioning, rather than tactical readjust-
ments, that would move South Africa from this scenario to
Scenario 5, and beyond.

This last point is conceptually valuable. What Africans
want, what the West calls for, and what a peaceful (or at
least noncataclysmic) solution to the South African problem demands is a major strategic shift of a kind that happens only very occasionally in the life of any modern state.
What governments in crisis generally try to do, instead, is
to evade strategic necessities by tactical rearrangements
and repositionings. An outside judgment is that only when
a party, a ruling oligarchy, or a government is prepared to
take the conceptual leaps that a strategic reassessment log-
ically demands will South Africa begin to address (and
therefore presumably to resolve) the fundamental issues of
a country where a decreasing minority denies effective political participation at the central (and other) levels to its
majority.

Concessions (5)

Scenario 5, Concessions, is not yet the scenario within
which South Africa is operating. Since Scenario 5 is different more in degree than in kind from Scenario 6, however,
South Africa could slide easily from the one to the other,
but not back. Part of the regime's current dilemma is that a
return to a Scenario 6 posture cannot be achieved once Scenario 5 has been entered. Thus, the transition from 6 to 5

worries the government. And 5 has an open-ended quality unsettling to any government bent more on cautious than wholesale reform, or, to put the proposition in a slightly different way, any government seeking to control the pace and direction of reform rather than to begin a process over which authority could be lost.

Under Scenario 5, which could prevail any day now, the levels of violence common during 1985, especially after the declaration of the state of emergency, would induce the government to grant concessions (meaningful to whites, as discussed above, but not to blacks), and then more concessions, and then further concessions – without achieving fundamental stability. What differentiates 5 from 6 and others is that the entrance into this scenario would be hastened by a combination of continued or renewed violence and intensified pressure from the West. The introduction of stronger U.S. sanctions, the animosity of Europe (and Australia and Canada), would be but a part of the overall atmosphere of Western alienation.

A second distinctive aspect of Scenario 5 is that the conferring of concessions would be preceded, in each case, by some form of consultation between the state and presumably "authentic" representatives of the protesting majority. Consultation had not occurred in any notable or easily legitimized degree by the time of President P.W. Botha's August 1985 "Rubicon" speech to the Natal Congress of the National Party. Indeed, the government may already have lost its final opportunities to consult by that time, inasmuch as Africans had moved on to demands for negotiated settlements and it had become dangerous to be consulted by the government. Any such consultation, by individuals or groups, risked a loss of credibility and the label "collaborator" or "stooge."

Nevertheless, it is theoretically possible for a government intent on believing that concessions would mute an opposition, or quiet protesters, to find Africans with whom discussions can occur. A government might also believe that the very contours of its concessions might defuse or defer protest. Clearly the government of South Africa could gain credibility overseas with the enunciation of an end to pass laws and influx control, broad new plans for housing and education, the introduction of an African franchise at the local or regional level, the provision of common citizenship, and so on. Nelson Mandela could be released. But such attempts to buy peace and time are bound to be insufficient if – from the majority point of view – they are introduced unilaterally and are not part of an overall restructuring of South Africa, including the homelands. In a more profound sense than most Africans realize, the majority seeks official recognition that South Africa can no longer progress without considering black preferences and opinions. Africans seek to become an integral part of the bargaining process.

Limited Power Sharing (4)

The government of South Africa has long ago realized that Africans prefer Scenario 4 to 5. That is, Africans want power sharing, even if limited, rather than concessions. The government would very much prefer to provide the latter, and to guide (a euphemism for control) the process. The government wants to slow down, to be static and passive. Those reactions are all possible under 5, but not 4. Thus the conceptual leap between 5 and 4 is much greater than between 6 and 5. Yet the failure of 6, Change But No Change, signaled by violence without end and the inability to repress without embarrassing losses of life, could lead to a decision to move directly from 6 to 4 – on the grounds that concessions would be refused or rebuffed, but that limited power sharing would have at least some chance of halting rioting and removing the sting of protest. This it might, but only if the shift to limited power sharing is negotiated with Africans. To decide to negotiate is the major step. To persuade Africans recognized as politically legitimate to negotiate is a second major move, and both are intertwined.

A result of open bargaining between whites with physical and economic power and blacks with numerical (and possibly historical) power could be the sharing of political control in the operational sense between white and black at local and regional levels. The black cities would become black-governed entities with full revenue-raising and revenue-expending powers. Blacks would receive the franchise at the municipal level. Municipalities would obtain statutory rights and also have influence at the regional level. Blacks would begin to experience autonomy – a measure of control over their destiny in the political sense. They would start to have a stake in their own country, and have real if limited power as against the central government.

It is within this scenario that the South African government could experiment with the devolution of regional authority or consociational arrangements. It could shift responsibility for black affairs, education, health, and so on to a new provincial government composed of black and white representatives, as proposed in the Ciskei Commission and Buthelezi Commission reports.

It is not clear whether or not the government has begun to think broadly and innovatively about limited power sharing in the sense of Scenario 4. Again, it is a question of power devolved being essentially unrecoverable. Further, although whites might be persuaded to concede limited power sharing in the sense described, they would want power sharing to remain limited, and not be a transitional stage. Africans, on the other hand, may have reached the point where they can only be persuaded to accept limited power sharing if they believe it to be a prelude to Scenario 3. Alternatively, but only after a period of bitter repression, Africans might become more willing to accept such "half loaves" rather than the full loaf that their leaders urge them to demand.

Scenario 4 would clearly become an option for the white government only after levels of violence reached new heights, Western pressure became even more insistent, and the National Party underwent substantial alterations in the nature of its leadership. A fundamental move would elevate those who believed in the modernization of white attitudes over those who preferred to react rather than gamble. Leaders would arise who understood that the old ways – the ways of the higher-numbered scenarios – simply cannot give South Africa stability and prosperity.

Power Sharing (3)

Scenario 4 is an alternative to 5, and not as likely a progression from 5 as it is from 6. Scenario 3, Power Sharing, obviously flows from 6, and could result directly (as could 2) from 6. If violence is high and sustained for long periods, if police and military repression proves insufficient to quell or shorten the cycles of violence, if Western pressure grows more compelling and isolating, if prosperity fades (for whites as well as blacks), and if – decisively – the costs to the white way of life as well as the country's economy become too great (or are so perceived by large numbers of whites), then Scenario 3 becomes an operational possibility.

A shift to 3 is less abrupt, by definition, than a shift directly to 2. But it would nevertheless occur with comparative rapidity once the decision makers appreciated that the white will to resist or to continue fighting had snapped. That appreciation would occur subjectively, not objectively, but it would occasion a crisis of legitimacy.

There are two preconditions: (1) that Africans would, over the bargaining table, be constrained to accept less than "one man, one vote" by the existence of a still strong military machine in white hands, and (2) that leaders would assume power in the National Party and in the top echelons of the Defense Force who were prepared to settle for less than total victory and to demand more than total defeat. Leaders of that caliber would not necessarily arise in time, or become conscious early enough to play their role. Nor would a military leadership necessarily recognize that there is an alternative between victory and defeat. Nevertheless, if there were unremitting agitation by Africans at levels five times greater than in 1985, white persons of power would be compelled to devise a new solution and Scenario 3 could be the negotiated result.

Substantial Regime Change (2)

Scenario 2 – Substantial Regime Change – is less than a revolution, for the prevailing order changes, but the structure of society remains. It may sound farfetched in the mid-1980s, but South Africa could be transformed radically and rapidly without the classical revolution which, as we have reasoned, is highly unlikely. Substantial regime change means a shift from white to majority rule under conditions of uncommonly high stress, with limited time for adjustment, little preparation, and few safeguards for minorities.

Scenario 2 could prevail if, after a period of sustained violence at about, say, 10 times the 1985 intensity, with widespread loss of white as well as black life, the white government finds that the quenching of violence is possible only by open negotiations with Africans from a posture of weakness rather than strength. Prior to this point a National Party regime would have given way to a transitional white group, the military would have acknowledged an inability to continue fighting in a sustained way against Africans, and partition would be the solution on the lips of many.

The Odds

These are the logical alternatives for the future of South Africa. A simple conclusion is that there is every cause for anxiety, since none of the scenarios is promising, and each of the possible states would be reached only by the compulsion of events, not imaginative leadership. On the other hand, the 1984–1985 cycle of violence does not necessarily and ineluctably presage repetitious cycles immediately. Historical determinism is not at work, but numerical superiority, international hostility, and the passage of time may nevertheless produce the same results.

8

A Fundamental Shift in South African Politics?

Ken Owen

January 1986

A South African newspaper editor, holidaying with the country's white elite at the coastal resort of Hermanus near Cape Town, was called from the beach to take an urgent telephone call. "Thabo here," said the caller. The voice was that of Thabo Mbeki, publicity secretary of the banned African National Congress, calling from Lusaka (Zambia) to make sure that the ANC's 18-page policy statement of January 8 was not misinterpreted.

A fundamental shift has occurred in South African politics during the past 18 months, bringing the African National Congress back to center stage after 25 years of precarious existence in exile. ANC colors – black, green, and gold – are flown everywhere. Newspapers report fairly freely on the strategies and purposes of the exiled leadership, and occasionally (either with permission from the government or at the risk of prosecution) ANC President Oliver Tambo is quoted directly. Universities offer public lectures on ANC strategy. At funerals, young blacks occasionally march with wooden replicas of that international symbol of revolution, the AK-47 Soviet assault rifle. Even Chief Buthelezi, the Zulu leader who claims the ANC is trying to assassinate him, has found it expedient to recall his old ties to

Nelson Mandela and to join in the demand for the ANC leader's release from Pollsmoor prison.

The reemergence of the ANC is more symptom than cause of the realignment of political forces that has, in a relatively short space of time, altered entirely the outlook for South Africa and shortened all its time scales. Marxists would speak of "a shift in the correlation of forces," but it is perhaps more accurate to say that 1985 saw a coalescence of forces, internal and external, that reinforced each other to confront white South Africans, for the first time, with identifiably revolutionary conditions.

The visible front rank of revolution consists mainly of "the youth," students and pupils ranging in age from 7 to 22 years, under the shadowy leadership of students or cadres aged between 20 and 40. The average age of township activist gangs — judged from the ages of the casualties at hospitals — has been put at 14. Most violence can be attributed to these gangs. But the struggle for liberation is as often carried forward by the churches, or by labor unions, or by lawyers in the courts and medical staff at the hospitals, or by the unemployed, or by community organizations, or by sudden informal alliances whose origins and organization cannot be traced.

Increasingly, even the solid black middle class has been drawn into the struggle. In other words, the black community has been thoroughly politicized on a scale never seen before in South Africa. While it would be misleading to suggest that these elements all pursue the purposes of the ANC, it is nevertheless fair to say that they are all heading in roughly the same direction and that their actions have become both mutually reinforcing and increasingly sharply focused. The degree of socialism in the liberation struggle is in dispute; the fact that socialists dominate and lead that struggle is not.

Nor should the external dimension be ignored. Incipient insurrection, captured on television and disseminated internationally, has elicited international pressures on such a scale as to demoralize important elements of the white community and thus to reinforce internal protest. The turbulence has caused an international failure of confidence in South Africa's future, undermining the value of the currency, and shattering the always fragile confidence of South Africa's own business elite. The most essential ingredient of capitalism — faith in the future — has evaporated.

By the end of 1985, ebullient ANC leaders were talking of a power seizure by 1990, and at least one major corporation had shortened its own political risk time scale for "possible" revolution to five years. This estimate is surely hysterical, given the weight of the rival forces, but very few informed people are still prepared to envisage 20- or 25-year scenarios. The past year has been too full of surprises to permit such confidence in prophecy. The rapidity of events has generated such momentum that it has become a task of daunting complexity to trace cause and effect.

A Framework for Analysis

The following sequence sets forth, if somewhat arbitrarily, a coherent framework within which the emergence of prerevolutionary or revolutionary conditions may be assessed:

(1) The reform program of the National Party, initiated after the riots of 1976 but stepped up sharply after the accession to power in 1978 of a *verligte* (enlightened) cohort led by President Pieter W. Botha, failed to stabilize the country as it was intended to do. On the contrary, it raised the expectations of the black population without being able to satisfy these expectations, while at the same time creating new avenues for protest and resistance to white rule.

In particular, the government's reform constitution, approved overwhelmingly by the white electorate in November 1983, had precisely the opposite of its envisaged effect. As many critics predicted, the very fact that it brought Indians and Coloureds into the new tricameral parliament, and did not make any reference whatsoever to the black majority, proved a major political blunder. Intended as a "step forward" in the reform process, the constitution was instead seen by blacks as another act of rejection and indeed as an attempt to co-opt the minority communities in an antiblack alliance. These suspicions were strengthened when the preelection promises of Allan Hendrickse and Amichand Rajbansi to use their positions within the cabinet to press for further change proved ephemeral once they took office. Reform proceeded, but at a pace set by the National Party caucus, not by its new allies.

(2) The Botha government's acceptance of the principle that there was need for reform acted as a spur to hope that the iron grip of apartheid could, at last, be broken. Black aspirations quickly outran any possible program of reform, rather than vice versa. In a classic first stage of revolutionary activity reminiscent of Algeria, the first victims were "collaborationists"—notably town councillors who had accepted office under the government's program of municipal reform, black policemen, and suspected police informers. Executions were public, horrifying, and (thanks to the government's more liberal attitude toward the international media) disseminated worldwide by television. In some cases, such as that of the township of Duduza on the East Rand, all policemen and their families were driven out and had to live in tents in the veld through a bitter highveld winter. Police dared not enter many areas, except in force, and township dwellers became wary of even acknowledging acquaintanceship with any policeman for fear of immolation.

(3) Beyond the execution of "sellouts" there was also a war of attrition between rival factions, mainly between the Azanian People's Organization (AZAPO) on one side and the United Democratic Front on the other, a conflict based on deep ideological differences. AZAPO is the main remnant of the Black Consciousness movement that swept the black communities in the early 1970s, culminating in the Soweto riots of 1976 and 1977 which left nearly 600 people dead.

Those riots, it warrants remembering, left the exiled leadership of the ANC astonished and dismayed: the long-awaited revolution seemed for a while to be starting without them. Since then, the ANC has spared no effort to reestablish its dominance against the challenge of the Black Consciousness organizations. In this, it found an ally in the United Democratic Front, formed in January 1983 as an umbrella for several hundred organizations representing all races. The government has accused the UDF of acting as a front for the ANC, which would be illegal, and the UDF has (for obvious reasons) denied the charge. All that can be said with certainty is that the ANC is not hostile to the UDF, and that many actions of UDF members have followed closely the script written by the ANC and broadcast from exile offices in Lusaka and Addis Ababa.

(4) Increasingly, the ANC (thanks in part to the sophisticated input of the South African Communist Party members who make up half its executive) has managed to preside over the entire process. The mistake of 1976, when ANC attention was so fixed on exile politics that it overlooked events on the ground inside South Africa, has not been repeated.

(5) The combination of mass demonstrations, an explosion here and there, public executions, school boycotts, and other activities gathered sufficient momentum to overwhelm the capacity of South Africa's small 42,000-man police force. Beginning in October 1984, with what is now known popularly as "the invasion of Sebokeng," units of the army had to be deployed. Even so, control could not be restored and the government was compelled by mid-1985 to formulate a new response.

(6) The response selected by President Botha was, probably from naivete rather than defiance, the worst possible option: the declaration as of July 21 of a formal state of emergency in 36 magisterial districts (out of 265 countrywide), permitting the government to invoke special powers over about a quarter of the population. These regulations,

inter alia, indemnified the police and the armed forces against civil or criminal suits for any action taken in good faith to deal with the emergency. They added little, however, to the existing powers of the government to deal with protests (indefinite detention without trial, gagging, house arrest, banishment, and scores of other arbitrary measures).

Emergency powers have one important feature lacking in the normal law: they require the government to account for its actions to parliament. It is possible, therefore, to speculate that the declaration of the state of emergency was a "liberal" rather than a "repressive" impulse – that it was a reformist Botha response to two decades of liberal criticism of the legislation that, in effect, entrenched similar emergency powers in the common law. A liberal impulse can in any event be discerned in the decision to allow the international media, including network television, free access to the areas of civil disturbance.

(7) The combination of the vivid phrase "state of emergency" and television proved deadly. The violence in the townships, which had been a fact of life for eight or nine months, was so dramatized by this combination that it created an international crisis of confidence in South Africa's future prospects. This in turn led to a flight of capital which was precipitated, so far as these things can be ascertained with any certainty, by a decision of the Chase Manhattan Bank not to roll over credits. As the word spread, other U.S. banks followed suit, and then banks in Europe, creating an unmanageable liquidity crisis. A small bank in West Germany, more panicky than the larger institutions, quickly put South Africa on the same list of countries as Uganda, thereby collapsing one Afrikaner businessman's plans for an import-based manufacturing venture.

(8) Although South Africa's foreign debts were relatively small (some $24 billion), it could not hope to meet what was effectively a run on the currency. The value of the rand, stable for many years at about $1.40 until it drifted to about parity with the dollar in the late 1970s, collapsed to less than $0.35 before recovering somewhat on a rise in the

price of gold. Despite its vaunted wealth, South Africa was forced to declare a moratorium on debt repayments – vastly inflated in terms of local currency as the value of the rand declined – and to reinstitute exchange controls on capital movements.

The plunging currency raised import costs – fuel, automobile components, and capital goods in particular – and thus ended any hope of rapid control of inflation or of early renewal of sustainable economic growth. By early 1986, inflation was running at the highest level in 66 years and fears of hyperinflation were real, if exaggerated. Major corporations lost fortunes as their dollar-denominated debts soared in rand terms; bankruptcies multiplied; many medium-sized firms closed down; and large employers laid off workers in thousands. Unemployment, already as high as 56 percent of the black working population in the Eastern Cape and high elsewhere, appeared insurmountable in the short run and probably in the long run. Lack of jobs, quickly identified as a major contributor to civil disturbance, was likely to remain so. The cycle of economic deprivation and political violence appeared to many observers to be fixed.

(9) There was one chance to turn the tide. President Botha was given an opportunity, when he addressed a party congress in Durban in August, to address simultaneously via television a large and well-primed international audience. Foreign Minister Roelof F. ("Pik") Botha, believing that the outlining of a credible program of reform could alleviate international pressure, flew to Europe to prepare especially the Americans and the British for a major reform announcement. Expectations were raised sky-high, as illustrated by Australia's decision to suspend consideration of sanctions and to call its ambassador from leave to provide an instant analysis of the speech.

(10) Faced with this matchless opportunity, President Botha fell victim to the small-town character of South African politics and to his own ignorance (born of isolation) of the world beyond the short Afrikaner horizon. Peeved that a briefing to Afrikaans newspaper editors had leaked and

found its way into the mildly antigovernment Johannesburg daily, *The Star*, he rewrote his speech and delivered
himself of a clumsy, finger-wagging display of belligerence
and bad temper. The reform section of his speech was
wrapped in local political jargon so obscure as to mystify
even most South Africans.

(11) The effect of this speech, dubbed Rubicon I, was
quite devastating. A major stockbroking firm in New York,
its chief executive appalled by the lack of leadership and
vision to be found in either text or manner of presentation,
promptly restricted its dealings in South African invest-
ments. Phibro-Salomon, one of the world's leading commodity dealers, decided to pull out. Holders of foreign pass-
ports, trapped inside the country by the weakness of the
currency that made emigration ruinous, became known
mockingly as "rand-locked." Even so, Johannesburg stock-
broker Harold Shapiro was so shattered by the speech that
he sold up and emigrated to Australia. Thousands of others
planned to follow. Confidence in the Botha government, internally and abroad, had quite literally collapsed. Even
some Afrikaners, albeit the modernist young, talked of
emigration.

(12) The government, meanwhile, resorted increasingly
to repressive measures in its attempts to restore order to
black communities. The number of people detained rose to
almost 7,000, including many leaders of the UDF and many
moderates. Some children as young as 14 were kept in detention for months. At least 11 people died in detention, or
soon after their release, raising again the specter of Steve
Biko and Neil Aggett, both of whom died after maltreat-
ment in police custody.

Television cameras were banned from unrest areas (with
the explanation that they stimulated riots), and print journalists were harassed or expelled. Instead, the course of
violence was chronicled in curt – and often inaccurate –
communiqués issued from police headquarters. These communiqués did, however, convey a gradual change in police
tactics: the bullwhips (*sjamboks*), rubber bullets, and shot-

guns loaded with birdshot that had horrified television audiences abroad were largely phased out. Youth gangs attacking black policemen were now more likely to come under gunfire and then flee after one or two of their number had been killed. The arming of black policemen was not new; however, the number of casualties that resulted suggested a new willingness to shoot to kill, at least in self-defense.

Whereas almost half the fatalities as of early 1985 could be ascribed to internecine violence among blacks, by the end of the year a huge majority of black deaths were caused by police action. The toll was high: 1,028 persons were reported killed between September 1984, roughly the beginning of the violence, and December 1985. Fewer than 20 of these fatalities were white.

(13) The number of politically related deaths in 1984–1985 was almost double the toll of the Soweto and post-Soweto violence of 1976, a period in which violence extended across the length and breadth of the country. A number of antiapartheid leaders and UDF supporters vanished, or were found killed. Some, such as lawyer Victoria Mxenge, were openly assassinated. Blame fell on police agents or on Inkatha, the Zulu cultural-political organization led by Chief Buthelezi. But there was reason to suspect a campaign of deliberate vilification of Inkatha as the UDF tried to move into Zulu territory in Natal.

Natal became the scene of bloody clashes between Inkatha and UDF factions, and this violence spilled into other areas of traditional hostility to encompass Indians and Pondo tribesmen from Transkei. The issue became even more confused when it turned out that at least one group of vigilantes called itself "Inkatha" even though it was not connected with Chief Buthelezi's organization, while Inkatha's enemies often applied the name to any Zulu, including policemen. Similarly, there seemed to be an element of propaganda in accusations leveled at a mysterious "third force," often likened to Latin American police death squads; here again the truth was not ascertainable.

(14) One element of the violence became increasingly clear: while the ANC claimed control over the township gangs (the groups it called "mass combat units" and cited as evidence of the emergence of the "People's War" phase of revolution), many of the youngsters were clearly under nobody's control. School boycotts persisted throughout the year, and matriculants were prevented from taking their exams. Many white families and some white private schools took in young blacks during the closing months of the academic year in order to permit them to continue their education without excessive danger; but for most pupils any attempt to take exams carried a risk of "burning," as death by fire came to be called.

A revolutionary euphoria took hold of the youngsters who, foreseeing the imminent overthrow of the government, adopted the slogan, "Liberation now, education later." Pupils in cohorts of as many as 200 roamed the townships enforcing revolutionary discipline and eliminating so-called "collaborators," usually by placing an old car tire around the victim's neck, filling it with gasoline, and setting it on fire.

One of South Africa's most capable black journalists, Aggrey Klaaste, described poignantly in the magazine *Frontline* how a group of children, neatly dressed in the school uniforms that are usual in South Africa, waited quietly in the street to kill a man — and did. Children of 14 armed with knives on occasion drove teachers out of classrooms and forced second-graders to burn their books. Consumer boycotts launched against white traders were enforced with considerable brutality. In some cases, for example, shoppers were forced to drink bottles of cooking oil or detergent; some died. A more positive effect of the boycotts was their role in persuading the business community to throw its weight into the campaign for political reforms.

In responding to the ANC's call to make "the country ungovernable, apartheid unworkable," the youth gangs constructed roadblocks, often of burning vehicles, and engaged the police forces by hurling stones and crude petrol bombs. Over time, more antipersonnel grenades were used against the police, and occasionally snipers took part. The police force, shaped by its duty to enforce apartheid laws that reduce blacks to subhuman status, responded with marked brutality and repressive zeal.

The ANC's New Strategy

In June 1985, the ANC held a major consultative congress at Kabwe in Zambia, near the site of one of its earliest training camps at Mkushi River. The decisions taken at Kabwe were confirmed in detail by the ANC's president, Oliver Tambo, at a press conference in Lusaka on January 9, 1986 (a year and a day after the ANC's initial broadcast instruction to make the townships ungovernable).

The Kabwe decisions reflected a new and assertive confidence that the South African regime could be displaced and that the time had come to push for power. The apartheid state was perceived to be in terminal crisis, its ideological base destroyed, its policies empty, and its options narrowing rapidly. To exploit this situation, the Kabwe meeting adopted a revised strategy focused on three areas of activity: expanded guerrilla war conducted by cadres; the "People's War" conducted under loose ANC direction by "mass combat units" (e.g., township youth); and a political campaign to isolate the Botha regime and widen the revolutionary base.

Guerrilla cadres in the field would be given more scope. Whereas the ANC previously had confined attacks fairly strictly to military or strategic targets (such as the Sasol oil-from-coal plant, or the Koeberg nuclear power station, or the offices of military personnel) and had sought to minimize or avoid civilian casualties, guerrillas were now authorized to attack any target of strategic significance, even if the attack might involve civilian casualties. On October 7, instructions were broadcast to cadres to attack whites in their suburbs and holiday resorts; by Christmas, the order had been fulfilled in a holiday attack on the white resort of Amanzimtoti.

In furtherance of the "People's War," emphasis was placed in the months after Kabwe on light training—often just to make petrol bombs or to throw hand grenades—for youngsters recruited inside South Africa. (In one pitiful series of episodes, seven young men had their hands blown off when their grenades exploded prematurely, leading to reports that a cache of arms had been found by the security forces and booby-trapped. An equal possibility is that the youngsters had misunderstood their instructions.)

Following the third Kabwe guideline, the ANC appealed for the first time to a wide range of other groups within South Africa to join a revolutionary (not simply a political) alliance. Trade unions, specifically the National Union of Mineworkers, were urged to strike; white conscripts were urged to resist military call-up; white businessmen were asked to turn down defense contracts; the churches were invited to join the struggle; and, of course, the township dwellers were asked to establish street committees as elements of a revolutionary government.

Showing increasing political confidence, Tambo engaged in direct contact with other opponents of apartheid. A delegation of liberal businessmen, led by the chairman of the Anglo American Corporation, Gavin Relly, met ANC leaders in Zambia, and was followed in quick succession by students, journalists, churchmen, and the Leader of the Opposition in the (all-white) House of Assembly, Dr. Frederik van Zyl Slabbert of the Progressive Federal Party. The Botha government stepped in to prevent Afrikaner students from the University of Stellenbosch and ministers of the Dutch Reformed Church from joining the procession.

The Other Side of the Coin

The ANC's confidence in the imminence of revolution, understandable in light of events in the townships (especially as depicted in the international media), is surely unrealistic.

It is inconceivable that the white ruling class will relinquish power and privilege before its armed forces are defeated, or at least severely tested. So far, that test has not come.

The ANC is reported to be able to draw on about 10,000 variably trained guerrillas, and it can rely on the support of hundreds of thousands of untrained and unarmed township dwellers. But the Botha government can call up at short notice an army of more than 400,000, many superbly trained and equipped for local conditions, to support a police force now being expanded to 65,000 men. (Black recruits for both military and police forces are not, incidentally, lacking; more applicants are still being turned away than accepted.)

Another development that must be taken into account is the emergence as 1985 drew to an end of some distinct signs of right-wing backlash within the white community. A series of by-elections showed, beyond any doubt, that the principal threat to the Nationalist government comes not from the moderate Progressive Federal Party on its left, but from the growing Conservative Party (and the even more extreme Herstigte Nasionale Party) on its right. Political inertia sustains for the moment the appearance of a National Party in full control, and may even do so through the next election, but it is already clear that Botha now depends for survival on a coalition of English-speaking and Afrikaner reformists.

The English-speaking constituency, insofar as it has ever existed as an entity, has now disintegrated under pressure. Socialism is attracting some young intellectuals into alliances with the UDF and similar organizations (it has become a fad for politically committed whites to work as officials for black trade unions). English-speaking liberals, among them many journalists who were demoralized by the closure of the *Rand Daily Mail* and the *Sunday Express*, have been emigrating in alarming numbers. The business community, unrepentant of its support for the disastrous constitution of 1983, still looks toward the Botha reformists as the best option and tries assiduously to influence them; and when its members lose hope, they too look to Australia or the United States as an escape.

On the other hand, the Afrikaner police and some elements of the army are bleakly critical of Botha's failure to contain the violence, which they attribute to a failure of will to govern. The same attitude is discernible in cruder form in the ranks of the civil service, the Afrikaner farming community, and the large Afrikaner artisan class. The civil service, in particular, has become a pivotal constituency, one which has proved immune to all Botha's attempts to reduce the size and weight of the bureaucracy.

A shift to the right in the cabinet over the tactics to be employed by the security forces is also clearly discernible. The decisions to take South Africa off the television screens of foreign countries, to invoke the state of emergency, and apparently (as mentioned earlier) to substitute sharp ammunition for rubber bullets and whips all reflect this harder line. The death in January 1986 of two young white policemen trapped by a mob of angry mineworkers did nothing to mitigate the trend.

In foreign policy too, the harder line is in ascendancy. The overthrow of the government of Prime Minister Leabua Jonathan in Lesotho in January 1986 was clearly precipitated by the unadmitted blockade that South Africa imposed on this landlocked country at the turn of the year. This sequence of events resulted in the expulsion of ANC cadres and refugees from Lesotho, and seemed to presage similar pressure on other neighbors. The Nkomati Accord with Mozambique, breached by the South African military in 1985 in connivance with the deputy foreign minister (who acted without the knowledge of the foreign minister), appeared shakier than ever before.

The key, however, is the economy. The exports of capital required to deal with the debt burden will absorb the fruits of growth for the next several years, or indeed well into the 1990s. The chance that South Africa might grow out of its trouble—so promising in the 1960s and early 1970s—has been squandered. A major government failure has been its

inability to curb its own burgeoning bureaucracy, and therefore its inability to manage the economy properly; there is
no political prospect that this situation can be reversed. On
the contrary, a powerful Afrikaner lobby has emerged under
the leadership of Fred du Plessis, chairman of Sanlam,
which argues for a reversion to the tight, centrally controlled economy that existed before the accession of the
relatively liberal Botha government. With or without sanctions, foreign economic involvement in South Africa seems
likely to decline.

Where Will It All End?

Meanwhile, the forces of violence, black and white, are visi-
bly gaining momentum as the reform constituency becomes
progressively more tattered. On the left, ideologues now
talk of the prospect of a "quasi-Bolshevik revolution," but it
hardly seems likely that the white regime will yield easily to
such a threat. In short, the unstoppable momentum of revolutionary fervor in the townships, increasingly directed by
the ANC, must at some point run into the immovable ob-
ject of the government's security forces. Nor is it conceiv-
able that Chief Buthelezi, with a million disciplined followers and a tribal base of nearly six million Zulus, will remain
passive if power seems to be shifting toward people who, he
believes, plan to kill him. Similarly, the small but significant police and armed forces of the "independent" Bantustans could conceivably come into play in defense of vested
interests, as indeed they have already done on a small scale
in Transkei, Ciskei, and Bophuthatswana.

These grim contradictions have prompted an increasing
willingness among major corporations as well as political
scientists to contemplate "gloom-and-doom" scenarios. The
worst of these, but in some ways the most likely, envisages
a gradual decline through economic stagnation and political
intransigence into endemic and savage conflict. Since that
process cannot continue indefinitely without resolution, the
prospect arises that each faction which is able to command

reasonable resources of power—the whites in the industrial areas and the main farming regions, the ANC in the townships, Inkatha in Zululand, and so forth—may establish de facto control of some or other part of the country.

Such a process would tend at best to forcible partition and at worst to an unstable cantonization of the country. The question that faces all South Africans now is whether they can find within themselves the resources to avert such an outcome. In any case, the events of the past year have shown quite vividly that interventions from abroad are as likely to be destructive as helpful.

9

People's Power: A Beginning, Not an End

Zwelakhe Sisulu

March 1986

We stand today at a crossroads in our struggle for national liberation. . . . In any struggle, it is extremely important to recognize the critical moment, the time when decisive action can propel that struggle into a new phase. It is also important to understand that this moment doesn't last forever, that if we fail to take action that moment will be lost. This moment has a number of important features:

- The state has lost the initiative to the people. It is no longer in control of events.
- The masses themselves recognize that the moment is decisive, and are calling for action.
- The people are united around a set of fundamental demands, and are prepared to take action on these demands.

Having said this, I want to strike a note of caution. It is important that we don't misrecognize the moment, or understand it to be something which it is not. We are not poised for the immediate transfer of power to the people. The belief that this is so could lead to serious errors and defeats. We are, however, poised to enter a phase which can lead to transfer of power. What we are seeking to do is to decisively shift the balance of forces in our favor. To do this we have to adopt the appropriate strategies and tactics, we

155

have to understand our strengths and weaknesses, as well as [those] of the enemy, that is, the forces of apartheid reaction.

Having said this, let us describe some of the main features of the current situation. The government introduced the state of emergency because it was losing political control. It hoped that the emergency would achieve two objectives: firstly, to stop the advances of the democratic movement, and to destroy the people's organizations which were taking control in various parts of the country. Secondly, it aimed to reinstitute the puppet bodies in the townships which had been destroyed since the Vaal uprising 10 months previously. Through this two-pronged attack, it hoped to regain control, regain the initiative, and impose its apartheid reforms on the people.

In fact, the state failed hopelessly in these objectives. Its brutal actions, and atrocities committed by the SADF [South African Defense Force] and SAP [South African Police], only angered the people more and mobilized them in ever-growing numbers. Puppet structures, instead of being restored, came under more widespread attack. In a number of areas people's organizations strengthened their structures and became more rooted in the masses. Struggle began to be waged in all corners of the country and new organizations sprang up daily. Where youth had previously waged the struggle alone, whole communities now involved themselves in united action against the regime.

Despite the heavy blows against our leaders and organizations, there was a real strengthening of the democratic forces, the people's camp; and a weakening of the forces of apartheid, the enemy camp.

Let us first look at the situation in the enemy camp. When the regime declared the emergency, all sections of the white ruling bloc supported it, in the belief that the resistance of the people would be crushed, paving the way for a Buthelezi-Muzorewa option. Barely one month later this appearance of unity had crumbled. Mass resistance had spread and taken new forms. The regime stood more isolated than ever before at the international level; and the economic crisis reached new proportions with the loss of investor confidence in the stability of the South African regime. . . .

The people heightened contradictions within the ruling bloc by strategies such as the consumer boycott. The regime became increasingly divided and unable to act as greater pressure built up, locally and internationally, to meet the people's demands. The divisions reached right into the cabinet itself, as sections of the government differed with each other on the correct way to deal with the situation. The SPCC [Soweto Parents Crisis Committee] initiative created public divisions between the SADF and SAP on the one hand, and the DET [Department of Education and Training] on the other; something which previously would have been unthinkable.

The initiative passed into the hands of the people. The ANC, in particular, became seen as the primary actor on the South African stage. Not only the people, but sections of the white ruling bloc, began to look to the ANC to provide an indication of future direction. . . .

When the emergency was declared, a situation of ungovernability existed mainly in two areas, the Eastern Cape and the East Rand. By the beginning of this year the situation was very different. Ungovernability had not only extended to far more areas. The people had actually begun to govern themselves in a number of townships. . . . Structures were built which would survive the period of the emergency and beyond it. In a number of townships, the area was split up into zones, blocks, and areas, each of which would have its own committee, and some townships developed street committees. . . .

For the first time in decades, our people took up the struggle in the rural areas. People in a number of bantustan areas challenged the so-called tribal authorities, and in some instances even replaced these bantustan sellouts with people's village councils. Areas which the enemy could previously rely on as zones of subservience and passivity were now being turned into zones of struggle. In the midst of the emergency, our people waged campaigns against these puppets in seven of the nine bantustans. Of course, the majority of our people in the rural areas have yet to challenge their oppressors. But the significance of these developments should not be underestimated. Every day this process is being furthered as more and more people in the rural areas take up the cudgels of freedom. . . .

This doesn't mean that the regime has no strengths and we have no weaknesses. If we overplay the regime's weaknesses and ignore their strengths we shall be fooling ourselves. More importantly, if we only concentrate on our strengths and ignore our weaknesses we shall commit serious errors. I have pointed to positive tendencies which have to be encouraged. But we must also be aware of the counter tendencies which threaten to reverse our struggle if we don't address them seriously. We need to consolidate, defend, and advance the gains we have made in this period. In this way, we can deepen the breakthroughs we have achieved in the various parts, thereby ensuring that temporary gains are transformed into fundamental and long-lasting features of our struggle. . . .

Ungovernability Is Not People's Power

Why do we use the slogan "Forward to People's Power"? Firstly, it indicates that our people are now seeing the day when the people of South Africa shall have the power, when the people shall govern all aspects of their lives, as an *achievable reality* which we are working toward. Secondly, it expresses the growing trend for our people to move toward realizing people's power *now*, in the process of struggle, before actual liberation. By this we mean that people are beginning to exert control over their own lives in different ways. In some townships and schools, people are beginning to govern themselves, despite being under racist rule. When our people kicked out the puppets from the townships, they made it impossible for the regime to govern. They had to bring in the SADF as an army of occupation. All they could do was to harass and use force against our people. But they couldn't stop the people in some townships from taking power under their very noses, by starting to run those townships in different ways. In other words the struggles which the people [have] fought, and the resulting situation of ungovernability, created the possibilities for the exercise of people's power. People exercised power by starting to take control in areas such as crime, the cleaning of the townships and the creation of people's parks, the provision of first aid, and even in the schools. . . .

There is a growing tendency for ungovernability to be transformed into elementary forms of people's power, as people take the lead from the semiliberated zones. In the bantustans, for example, struggles against the tribal authorities have developed into struggles for democratic village councils. These councils are actually taking over in some areas, thereby adapting the forms of people's power developed in the townships to rural conditions. We must stress that there is an important distinction between ungovernability and people's power. In a situation of ungovernability, the *government* doesn't have control. But nor do the people. While they have broken the shackles of direct government rule, the people haven't yet managed to control and direct the situation. There is a power vacuum. In a situation of people's power, the *people* are starting to exercise control.

An important difference between ungovernability and people's power is that, no matter how ungovernable a township is, unless the people are organized, the gains made through ungovernability can be rolled back by state repression. Because there is no organized center of people's power, the people are relatively defenseless and vulnerable. Removal of our leadership in such situations can enable the state to reimpose control. . . .

Struggles over the past few months demonstrate that it is of absolute importance that we don't confuse coercion, the use of force *against* the community, with people's power, the collective strength of the community. For example, when bands of youth set up so-called "kangaroo courts" and give out punishments, under the control of no one, with no democratic mandate from the community, this is *not* people's power. This situation often arises in times of ungovernability. We know that this type of undisciplined individual action can have very negative consequences. When disciplined, organized youth, together with other older people, participate in the exercise of people's justice and the setting up of people's courts, when these structures are acting on a mandate from the community and are under the democratic control of the community, this is an example of people's power. . . .

A very important, almost astonishing, achievement of our people in this regard has been in the area of crime control. Apartheid and crime make very good bedfellows. They thrive on each other. In fact, very often it is difficult to tell them apart! But people's power and crime cannot coexist. I am not saying this lightly. Crime has thrived in all townships in the country. But in the areas where people are taking control, crime is being wiped out. This shows that the people do have the power, if we stand united in action. We can achieve things we would otherwise never imagine possible – if we are organized, if we use our collective strength. Where we have developed people's power we have shown that the tendency for one section of the community to lead, while the others remain passive, can be overcome. Therefore, those initiatives which overcome these divisions and bring our people together must be jealously guarded and developed to their full potential. The National Education Crisis Committee is one such initiative. . . .

The Struggle at Community Level

Any tactic that is likely to be sustained and to help build our organization, that consolidates our strength and our unity, must be encouraged. Any tactic that hampers this process must not be embarked on. Against this background let us look at recent campaigns.

In many townships, community councillors have been forced to resign. We have noted that popular structures have often been erected to replace them. Through these democratic organs, our people are starting to control their own lives. These organs are based on and simultaneously facilitate the development of organization.

In many townships, especially in the Transvaal, successful rent boycotts have been instituted. Some of these have been sustained for more than two years. The value of rent boycotts is that they strike at the material basis of Black Local Authorities, while simultaneously relieving some of the economic pressures on the masses. Without drawing exorbitant rents from our people, the community council system cannot operate. It is reported, now, that every month that the boycotts continue, the system is losing R2 million. Amongst our people, unemployment has reached a record figure and continues to increase. . . . In this situation, the people, by refusing to pay rent, transfer part of the burden to the system.

In the rural areas, bantustan rule is under sustained attack. So-called tribal authorities are being forced to resign and are sometimes being replaced by village councils that enjoy confidence and ensure the participation of the community.

One of the key forms of struggle employed in recent years has been the consumer boycott. The weapon's potency lies in the fact that it requires the organization of the entire community in order to be effective. . . . Its success in the Eastern Cape lay in the street committees which facilitated the effective participation of most residents. This proved very effective in the Eastern Cape in the people's campaign to get the troops out of the townships. Where organization has been weaker, the consumer boycott has not only been less successful, but its implementation has sometimes weakened rather than strengthened unity amongst the people. In such situations, young people, often well-meaning, have tended to apply force instead of political

education, to persuade the community to support the boycott. This has had the effect of alienating some people from
the struggle.

Another dramatic and often-utilized weapon is the stay-
away. Where it is based on strong organization, it is powerful and builds unity not only within the community, but
also between community and trade union organizations.
Where such organization is not present, where such stayaways are not adequately prepared, they tend to produce, as
with consumer boycotts, intimidation instead of persuasion, disunity instead of growing unity of the people. The
adequate preparation for such a tactic requires careful discussion amongst all sections of the community, including
hostel dwellers, and especially between community and
worker organizations. Only then is this weapon powerful
and effective.

A crucial demand of the entire African people remains
the abolition of the pass system. Sensing the continued
popular anger and militancy, Comrade Barayi, president of
COSATU [Congress of South African Trade Unions], made
a call at the launch of the trade union federation, for the
burning of the badges of slavery. Should such a call be implemented it is likely to capture popular imagination, to
involve every section of the African community and enjoy
the support of all democrats. . . .

Planning for the Future

When planning our future, we need to ask ourselves how do
we deepen and broaden this national unity? In assessing
different strategies, we need to ask ourselves whether they
will reach out to communities not yet touched by our organizations, particularly those in the rural areas, bantustans,
and small towns. We need to ask ourselves what actions,
campaigns, and strategies will overcome the uneven level of
development of our organizations in different areas. In
short, what action will pave the way for us to take even

greater strides forward in all sections of the community, in all areas.

We also need to examine ways of making inroads into the white community. To break the stranglehold that apartheid education has on the minds of white children. We must show their parents that apartheid education provides no future for their children, or any of South Africa's children.

A significant achievement of [the National Education Crisis Committee] was its ability to begin building alliances between different sections of our oppressed people: between parents and students, between students and teachers, between parents and teachers. This has laid the basis for undermining the divisions which the state tried to create between youth and older people, between urban and rural communities, between professionals and other members of the community. We have already given examples of the achievements of these alliances so far. But we know that the bonds between these different sections of the community could be strengthened still further.

There are still areas where students are fighting the education struggle without the support of their parents or teachers. There are still areas where the struggle is led by the youth and the students and older members of the community are left behind or alienated. There are still sections of the teaching profession who side with the apartheid government and promote its will. The question we face is how to strengthen the alliance between parents, teachers, and students. We will not defeat apartheid while the youth alone carry on the struggle against Bantu Education or other aspects of racist rule. We will not win while our ranks are split by teachers who have not yet thrown in their lot with the democratic movement. We will not win while parents remain alienated from the demands of their children. These weaknesses and divisions will only delay our victory.

Our task is to deepen the alliance between all sections of the community against Bantu education and all aspects of apartheid rule. It is to look for strategies which continually strengthen and enlarge the ranks of the people and constantly weaken, divide, and isolate the ranks of the enemy. . . . We must remember that the enemy is not sleeping while we plan our activities. We know that it openly attacks us. But it does not only operate outside our ranks. It also operates from within our ranks. From within, the enemy takes advantage of any sign of indiscipline, any disunity, every sign of weakness. It does this in order to confuse our people, to increase disunity, and sow chaos in our ranks. . . .

Our task is not only to build democratic organization[s], but to build these in such a way that they can withstand the harassment of the apartheid government. We know that our greatest strength lies in the power of the people, in our mass-based committees in the schools, streets, and factories, in our coordinated strength in our national organizations, such as NECC. . . .

(Excerpted from Mr. Sisulu's keynote address to the National Education Crisis Committee conference held in Durban in March 1986)

10

South Africa:
A Reporter's Notebook

John de St. Jorre

July 1986

I first came to South Africa 20 years ago to report a funeral. Passing quickly through Johannesburg, noting little else except the racial hierarchy outside of the old Lansdowne Hotel—white head porter, Indian deputy, and blacks carrying the bags—I drove to Pretoria.

The town was then small, dominated by its government buildings, its churches, and its Afrikaner heroes frozen in bronze. The streets were full of white faces. The funeral ceremonies took place on time, the *volk* mourned, and Dr. H. F. Verwoerd was laid to rest. My copy went off to *The Observer* in London, efficiently despatched by white telex operators. I zipped up my typewriter, packed my bag, and caught the next flight back to Lusaka, to Africa.

Reflecting on the experience in Zambia, I couldn't quite work out where I had been. I had spent four years in West, Central, and East Africa and I had undoubtedly just added another point to my continental compass. But what I had seen didn't look, smell, or sound like Africa.

It wasn't quite European either: there had been many black and brown faces in the background and the sun was different. The Afrikaners, though white, were different too. South Africa, as a name, was no great help. Perhaps a new name was needed, something like "Afrikania."

It was not until a decade later that I returned for much longer and wrote a small book about the country. Since then I have been back and forth, culminating in a six-week trip earlier this year.

Much has changed; much hasn't. But what I failed to see in 1966, South Africa's "African-ness," is now threatening to burst through the brickwork of its non-African facade.

The first thing that any foreigner learns about South Africa is that nothing is quite as he or she expected it to be, and that, although the bedrock obsession is the racial divide and the struggle for power, things are not always black and white.

What, in the refracted gaze of the outsider, is new over the last decade, and what isn't?

The most profound change by far is the mood of the blacks. There is a feeling of buoyancy, expectancy, and confidence that I believe is quite new. It is, moreover, based on achievement rather than on fantasy. For 21 continuous, bloody, costly months, South Africa's blacks have sustained a physical protest against the government and brought the centuries-old struggle for power to a new threshold.

This has happened notwithstanding the enormous disparity between State and black power, the regional differences, and the severe intra-black divisions. That this herculean effort has caused barely a ripple on the placid surface of white society is not as important as it might seem. Black power, "people's power," is at this stage essentially black therapy.

"Last year was the watershed," said Professor Chabani Manganyi, one of South Africa's few black clinical psychologists. "There was a dramatic broadening of resistance, and blacks finally broke the psychological barrier of thinking that the whites were all-powerful and could not be challenged. In 1976, it was a children's war. Now everyone is involved."

What matters for blacks is that the old fears, docility,

and inferiority complex have largely been exorcised. There is also the gut feeling that, after countless defeats and false dawns, and the knowledge that there is still a long road to travel, the end is in sight.

"We are not poised for the immediate transfer of power," said Zwelakhe Sisulu in the keynote speech at the National Education Crisis Committee's meeting in Durban in March 1986, in what is probably the best black analysis of the crisis to date. "We are, however, poised to enter a phase which can lead to transfer of power."

How do they know that? How do we know that they know? Knowledge in these cases is not a precise science. There are no elections, no reliable polls, no visible weakening of white power or will, no negotiations, no talks about talks to tell you what is blowing in the wind. But if you have been to South Africa before and go there now, you will know.

During my recent trip I sampled a township funeral (Alexandra), a Methodist prayer meeting in the heart of Johannesburg, a United Democratic Front rally in Cape Town, a shanty town fighting a removal in the Eastern Cape, and a liberation theologian's Easter church service in Soweto.

These gatherings have many things in common. First, there is a surprising cross-section of individuals, organizations, classes, and races engaged in what is simply known as "the struggle." Second, everything is intensely political; and while the immediate issues are probably local, the national agenda of ending apartheid and moving to black rule is never forgotten.

Third, there is an emotional undercurrent which carries with it a grittiness and pride I had not experienced before. This is evident in everyday demeanor. At Jan Smuts airport, I asked a black cleaning lady the way to the bank. "First we greet," she said firmly. Chastened, I made amends. "Good morning," she replied. "Now, the bank is on the next floor."

Finally, a sense of already living in another country – a

new, predominantly black South Africa—is inescapable.
Every meeting ends with that most moving of songs, billed
simply as the "national anthem" that has nothing to do with
Die Stem. *Nkosi Sikelele i'Afrika*, everyone sings, "God
Bless Africa."

Unity of spirit does not conceal disunity of method.
Black divisions are manifest in the banners that advertise
the UDF, the ANC, AZAPO, the South African Communist
Party (the *Soviet* Communist Party, at the Alexandra funeral last February), the different trade union federations, and
a host of local groups.

At the end of the celebrations marking the fifth anni-
versary of the Ulundi Choral Society, watched by a benign
Chief Buthelezi and the KwaZulu/Inkatha establishment,
everyone also sang *Nkosi Sikelele i'Afrika* (without the
clenched fists), yet the gulf between Inkatha and the other
black nationalist groups is wide and widening.

It is true, also, that there is no national black leadership in South Africa today. There is a lack of cohesion in
black politics that is both a source of strength and weakness. The tendrils of black resistance have been forced by
government repression to grow downwards instead of up-
wards, strengthening black power at the local level but dif-
fusing it nationally.

Yet the standing of the ANC has been dramatically
enhanced over the last 18 months despite it being officially
banned and regarded by the government as the devil incar-
nate. Its status is reinforced for the visitor in many, often
curious, ways.

These include the ANC flags and colors at every black
meeting; the steady flow of people to Lusaka—South Africa's equivalent of the Road to Damascus; the constant public debate about the wisdom or folly of the government
dealing with the organization; the telephonic chitchat that
goes on between the ANC and the journalists and others
("just pick up the phone and call Thabo Mbeki if you want
to go to see him," advised a journalist friend when I was
leaving for Lusaka); even Inkatha sports ANC colors and

Chief Buthelezi makes a careful distinction between his condemnation of the "External Mission of the ANC" and his amicable relationship with Nelson Mandela.

Mandela himself, the ANC's imprisoned leader, remains as potent as Banquo's ghost. No leader has emerged to usurp his place, and no settlement of black and white differences, or intra-black rivalries, is likely in his absence. If the struggle goes on for a long time, as it probably will, new black leaders will almost certainly emerge within the country, rather than from the older group of political prisoners and exiles.

But what is more striking than black divisions is the similarity of blacks' political goals. Look across the spectrum from homeland leaders like Chief Buthelezi and Enos Mabuza of KaNgwane, who recently had a red carpet reception by the ANC in Lusaka, to the UDF, the unions, to AZAPO and the black consciousness groups. All agree that the entire apartheid structure, including the Population Registration Act, the Group Areas Act, and segregated education, must go.

All demand, as essential conditions for a dialogue with the government, the release of Mandela and the political prisoners, the unbanning of the ANC and PAC, and freedom to organize and engage in open political activity. Only then can discussions begin on what they all describe as a nonracial, democratic, united South Africa—in short, a totally new political and constitutional order.

Black organizations tend to be vague about their vision of the future economic structure of the country, but there is a strong underlying assumption that there will be a major redistribution of wealth, with or without socialism.

Against this, the government's plans—and the white electorate's tolerance—for change appear totally inadequate. And here the two South Africas look as hermetically sealed, and as out of step, as they have been for much of their history.

There have, of course, been considerable changes during the last decade or so. But there are several important tests that have to be made to discover the true quality of "change" or "reform." First, the point of view. A glance through the black prism will produce a very different result from that seen from the white perspective.

From the black point of view, there have been four major changes – a steady increase in wages and skills, legalized trade unions, a recognition of permanence in so-called white areas, and the recent repeal of the pass laws. The rest – desegregating first-class hotels, parks, some beaches, repealing the Mixed Marriages and Immorality Acts and so on – is cosmetic.

Then there is the agent of change. Blacks' new position in the economy came largely as the result of economic growth and a shortage of skilled (white) labor. The recognition of black trade unions and leasehold rights was pressed on a reluctant government by the business community and a few enlightened individuals. The government deserves credit for finally getting to grips with the pass laws but blacks tend to see this as a response to over a year and a half of protest, violence, and pressure.

Finally, there is the matter of timing. At best, the government is seen as a reluctant reformer, reacting to events rather than initiating change because apartheid is inherently wrong. I remember Robert Sobukwe, the PAC leader rusticated in Kimberley, telling me in the wake of the Soweto upheaval in 1976 that if the government made three key social and economic reforms – education, pass laws, and housing – he risked losing massive support because these were the issues that most concerned blacks in those days. By implication, the ANC was likely to suffer the same fate.

At worst, the government is seen as a good gardener. "Pretoria is a pruner," said Fikele Bam, the black lawyer. "It prunes the apartheid tree to increase its strength."

The government reforms by stealth; often there is a step forward followed by a nervous step back. Reforms are announced but implemented after long delays, like the desegregation of the central business districts, or the granting of freehold rights to blacks in the townships, or the

restoration of citizenship which still leaves several millions—those who are deemed to belong to the nominally independent homelands—in limbo.

There has been a mighty change in the government's rhetoric as a result of the National Party sloughing off its right wing, its ideology, and a good chunk of its past. *Verligtheid*, once an unorthodox and rather daring left-wing philosophy, is now party gospel.

Phrases like "apartheid is dead," "universal suffrage in a unified South Africa," "power sharing," "outlawing hurtful discrimination" (is there another kind?), and "equal opportunities for all racial groups" strike the time traveler forcibly. A major reeducation program of the white community is under way.

To the government's credit, it has convinced itself and the majority of whites that a less rigid racially defined society is both acceptable and necessary. The result is evident in sport, in the lowering of racial barriers as blacks advance into the economy, in some levels of social contact, and in general attitudes. Whites are neither as arrogant nor blacks as servile as they used to be.

An Afrikaner civil servant explained it in generational terms. "My father, a retired inspector of black schools, has left the National Party to join the Conservatives," he said. "I am a loyal Nat and think P.W. Botha is doing the right thing in working toward a multiracial government through the tricameral Parliament, the Regional Services Councils, and so on. I admit though I still have the old hang-ups about blacks. But my son is quite different. He doesn't want to live with them but he treats them like anyone else, like human beings."

Nevertheless, South Africa remains two distinct racial cultures. Apartheid has done its work well and the results cannot be rapidly undone, particularly because the government is adept at shielding its constituency from the costs and unpleasantness inherent in real change.

"The government has been successful in persuading the bulk of whites that change is necessary and the Nationalists are the only people that can do it," said Professor Robert Schrire of Cape Town University. "It has also convinced whites that change will not affect their status, security, or living standards."

To an outsider, the country's whites appear to continue to live in their velvet-cushioned dream world. The sun shines, the maid comes to work, the cricket season gives way to the rugby season, foreign travel is a bit more difficult due to those treacherous foreign bankers who have sunk the rand; but it'll be a Mercedes or a BMW next year and the Natal beaches are always fun.

And then there's the South African Broadcasting Service. I love, in a masochistic way, listening to the English service of the radio where white South Africa's trivial pursuits are on daily public display. During my last visit I heard a heated debate on whether white children should wear school uniforms or not, the relative merits of zips over buttons on men's trousers, parlor games based on BBC models but embarrassingly bad, the plummy, more-British-than-the-British tones of the announcers retailing the endless weather forecasts and stock market reports, the oily smugness of the Radio Today Commentary, and the curious news values. Once, I sat up in bed with a jolt when a news item began " . . . a report into the recent unrest and violence has blamed the police . . . ," but it turned out to be about a riot in Birmingham.

Lionel Abrahams, the writer, put it well in a recent issue of the South African magazine *Leadership*. While cherishing the English cultural component of South Africa's heritage, he wrote: "I have little patience for the trivia and trash of English popular culture, and especially so when these are displacing indigenous matter to sustain the cozily evasive, half-mad myth that we are somewhere else."

That's it: many white South Africans seem to think they are in another country where their gilded lives are not overshadowed by the awesome knowledge that they share the land with black people, who outnumber them five to

one, and who desperately want a slice of what they take for granted – nice housing, good schools, clean, orderly, safe towns, and a vote to make sure the government stays in line and keeps things that way.

Other things that haven't changed: the charm and basic honesty (when you push them) of the Afrikaners; the friendliness of the blacks; the intense religiousness of all South Africans – surely one of the most churchgoing people on earth; the enduring illusions of whites that they "know" *their* (giveaway word) blacks; the newspaper editorials urging "change before it is too late" (they were writing that 10 years ago); the blank masks people wear as they pass others of a different race in the street; the sheer old-fashioned feel of South Africa (World War II nostalgia, and cigarette advertisements on the radio like the one for Peter Stuyvesant – still, hard to believe – the "passport to smoking pleasure"); the endless political talk, and white guilt, skin-deep but not about to be purged by giving up a good thing – at least, not yet.

So what, as American businessmen are fond of asking, is the bottom line?

There is a sense of expectancy in the air that was not apparent to me in 1966 or even in 1976. There is a long haul ahead but the country's "brawling constituencies," in journalist Ken Owen's phrase, seem to be strengthening their defenses and getting ready for the fray.

I do not have the impression that a negotiating – or even a pre-negotiating – climate exists. For the blacks, the balance of power isn't right; they would be negotiating at a severe disadvantage. For the whites, notably the Afrikaners, the costs are too low. Why concede anything of substance when you are not hurting and when, moreover, the alternative – black rule – is so frightening?

Yet the blacks, despite their relative powerlessness and isolation, have seized the initiative. Their agenda is very different from the government's. They are not talking about economic and social reform or cautious, government-controlled schemes to "share power" in complicated consociational structures dreamt up by Chris Heunis and his not untalented coterie of constitutional engineers.

"We are not fighting and dying in order to have a better system of waste disposal," Oliver Tambo commented recently on the new Regional Services Councils.

"The issue is not reform any longer," said Professor Deon Geldenhuys, "it is the struggle for power."

Some whites know this and have accepted it. They have truly crossed the only Rubicon that matters in South Africa and are now actively involved on the side of the blacks.

"Young people are aware that a change of consciousness, of the white sense of self, has to be achieved along with a change of regime, if, when blacks do sit down to consult with whites, there is anything to talk about," Nadine Gordimer wrote recently.

For whites – young, middle-aged, or old – who have crossed that threshold, the surge of black power is a unique, exciting experience.

"I wouldn't live anywhere else," said a member of the Black Sash. "When you go to a funeral or any event in the townships, you see black, brown, and white sharing the most exhilarating comradeship. Then I go back to my white suburb and feel like crying because I have left part of myself behind where the true South Africa is. It's inspiring and heartbreaking. But I wouldn't miss it for anything. You feel you are living history every day."

For anyone, South African or foreigner, who hasn't shared that feeling, the journey, in the words of the *Guide Michelin*, is worth the detour.

11

Sanctions: Another View

Michael Spicer

September 1986

The calls for various forms of economic sanctions against South Africa focus mainly on the immorality of apartheid. The frustration and despair that give momentum to the drive for sanctions are understandable, but serious strategists must take into account the historical record of sanctions situations in evoking a certain well-defined pattern of state and individual behavior. Some of the classic characteristics of the early phase of this pattern are already manifesting themselves in South Africa:

1. Xenophobia

The increased threat of sanctions in the wake of the May 1986 collapse of the Commonwealth's Eminent Persons Group (EPG) initiative has given an unpopular government, under growing pressure from many quarters, an opportunity to rally a widened spectrum of the white electorate into the laager in the cause of opposing what is increasingly perceived as misguided or irrational external pressure. Opinion polls conducted in the past few weeks indicate that the popularity of State President P.W. Botha has grown significantly among whites. If an election is called (and indications are that this may occur in the first half of 1987), the campaign mounted by the ruling National Party will be in a pseudopatriotic mode calculated to garner support from elements of the Progressive Federal Party on the left as well as the Conservative Party on the right.

In the shift to a siege mentality, Pretoria has not just turned its back on the steps which the international community has deemed the irreducible minimum (releasing Nelson Mandela, unbanning the African National Congress, and entering negotiations with legitimate black political leaders). It has also begun to slow down implementation of its own projected reform program. This slowdown appears to have been reactive rather than strategic, but it now seems likely that major reforms will remain on a back burner while the government focuses on two new priorities – solidifying its position through the white elections and getting the various dimensions of a counter-sanctions program in place.

As recently as May 1986, observers were confidently predicting the demise of the Group Areas Act within 18 months, with the President's Council playing a leading role in hastening this process. Not only has the President's Council report on the Act been delayed, but the National Party, divided on the issue, seems to be hardening its stance in anticipation of an early election.

2. The Mediator Vacuum

Beyond strengthening the government and delaying the process of limited but incremental change, the sanctions campaign has intensified racial polarization in South Africa. Opinion polls early in 1986 indicated a growing willingness among whites to contemplate the release of Nelson Mandela and talks with the ANC. Over time, however, new threats of sanctions, combined with government accusations of ANC violence and emphasis on the role of Communists in the ANC executive, have rendered whites more reactionary in their positions.

Many blacks, on the other hand, are understandably impassioned and frustrated by the slowness of reform and the obscurity of its objectives. Those in the West who encourage a mythology that sanctions can quickly usher in a radically new society respectful of human dignity and responsive to pressing basic needs will only heighten the frustrations. Understating the longer-term costs of sanctions or creating the illusion that these costs will be offset by massive Western aid hardens positions and undercuts opportunities for negotiation and compromise. The EPG's rigid timetable and the threat of additional sanctions implicit in the timetable acted in the end to rigidify the positions of both Pretoria and the ANC.

The sanctions issue has also distracted potential mediators within South Africa. Black trade unionists, faced by the specter of sanctions becoming a reality, increasingly take the position that business has a duty to keep workers in employment. The business community's response is that it can only do this if sanctions are avoided or evaded. The considerable energy that will go into this standoff will inevitably be lost to the search for political solutions.

3. Loopholes

Whatever the degree of international backing for sanctions, there is no reason to suppose that international compliance would be much greater than in previous sanctions situations.

Predictably, the nine member states of the Southern African Development Coordination Conference were unable to reach agreement at their meeting in Luanda in late August on implementation of the Commonwealth sanctions. SADCC appears to be splitting into hard-line and pragmatic camps on the issue, mainly but not exclusively according to the degree of their economic dependence on South Africa. The "hard-line" group would include Zimbabwe and Zambia, though President Kaunda's recent statement at the Nonaligned Summit in Harare (that sanctions imposed by Zimbabwe and Zambia on their own, without similar action by South Africa's major trading partners, would be "suicide" and "meaningless") suggests that Zambia may be having second thoughts. The "pragmatic" group would include Botswana, Mozambique, Malawi, Lesotho, and Swaziland. Mauritius, though not a SADCC state, falls clearly in the latter category.

Beyond southern Africa, other loopholes are immediately apparent, and each day brings more evidence of preparations to exploit them. Neither Taiwan nor Switzerland is a member of the United Nations and neither is likely to adhere fully to sanctions. The role of Soviet bloc and various Asian countries in helping "bust" Rhodesian sanctions in the 1970s also springs to mind. And despite some recent controversy in Israel over the extent of trade, technology, and security ties with South Africa, it is highly unlikely that there will be more than token restrictions on the many individual, corporate, and parastatal arrangements now in effect between the two countries. Efforts by the U.S. Congress to attach penalty clauses to legislation directed at U.S. aid recipients seeking to benefit from sanctions seem likely to elicit little beyond a more careful surface pretense on the part of various actors that trade bans are being observed.

4. The Economic Attrition Backlash

Some of the most ardent proponents of sanctions have come to recognize that, given the resilience of the South African economy and the determination of whites to resist sanctions, economic attrition as well as increased political violence will be inevitable if the absolutist agenda is to be met. The effects of the financial sanctions imposed by the international market in 1985 suggest that extended economic attrition would have major implications for postapartheid South Africa.

None of the financial sanctions currently being considered by the United States or the EEC threatens anything like the damage already sustained by the South African economy from the drying up of foreign capital inflows, the export of considerable amounts of the existing South African capital stock, and the disinvestment of a number of multinational companies, mainly from the United States. Yet, as is now abundantly evident, these traumas did not lead Pretoria to accelerate its reform program.

The imposition of formal bans on new investment would simply ratify a step which the market has already taken and which the South African economy has survived, albeit at a price. From 1964 to 1974, foreign capital provided 10 percent of South Africa's investment needs; gross domestic product growth averaged nearly 5 percent per annum. In the following decade, there was no net capital inflow; in fact, South Africa had to draw on reserves to achieve a growth rate only half that of the previous decade. Since 1980, real GDP growth has averaged only 1.1 percent per annum, and capital outflows reached a peak in 1985, when over R10 billion left the country.

Given South Africa's population growth rate (2.3 percent overall, 2.8 percent for blacks), any event which makes it more difficult to obtain a high growth rate will also contribute to a burgeoning unemployment rate. In fact, it is commonly held that a 5 percent GDP growth rate is needed to keep unemployment just at present levels. Moreover, companies that disinvest and markets and jobs that are lost may not return for decades (if at all) after apartheid has gone; damage to the economy will be enduring.

Pretoria can mitigate this trend to some extent by altering its economic strategy. Encouraging urbanization, emphasizing the job-creating potential of mass housing programs, and stimulating the informal sector and small businesses are among the options. Boosted by rising platinum and gold prices, the economy is currently showing signs of a modest recovery – though with almost all fundamentals such as consumer demand and investment growing from a low base.

It is perhaps too early to attribute much of a role to import substitution, but the Rhodesian experience is instructive. Although import replacement strategies necessitated by sanctions might provide short-term alleviation, they would skew the pattern of economic development away from its optimal course. In the South African case, much of the accent of both public and private investment would fall for strategic reasons on capital-intensive projects such as the Mossel Bay gas project, rather than on desperately needed labor-intensive developments. There would also be continuing erosion of South Africa's skills base as whites emigrated in increasing numbers and a return to the dramatic decline in gross domestic fixed investment witnessed over the past five years. In the long run, these trends would result in restricted job opportunities for generations of South Africans, black and white.

5. Wing-Clipping

The ending or restriction of landing rights for South African Airways would leave South Africans more reliant on airports in neighboring countries and unable to fly directly to the United States and perhaps Western Europe. One of the aims of such a measure, articulated recently by Australia's Malcolm Fraser, cochairman of the Commonwealth EPG, is to give the Republic's neighbors some leverage against the threat of South African counter-sanctions.

While anti-SAA measures would undoubtedly inconvenience those South Africans (mostly white) who travel overseas, wing-clipping sanctions would also encourage a sense of isolation and defiance rather than more rapid social and political change. Contingency plans already made by

SAA with neighboring governments would reduce some of the cost in lost earnings and lost jobs. White South Africans would adapt.

If migrant workers from Lesotho and Mozambique are eventually repatriated, the reason will be rising unemployment in South Africa — not a counter-sanction ploy.

6. Trade Sanctions Fallout

Trade sanctions, such as ending imports of South African agricultural products, coal, iron, steel, uranium, and gold coins, would involve the greatest economic cost to Pretoria — and to black South Africans as well.

All of these commodities are vulnerable to boycotts, given existing levels of surpluses. (It is noteworthy that some of the most ardent proponents of trade sanctions, e.g., Australia, would stand to gain some of South Africa's present markets.) Except for iron ore, South Africa would be able on current estimates to hold on to at least half to two-thirds of its existing export markets if trade sanctions were imposed. A far more immediate result would be job losses.

If a total ban on the importation of South African iron, steel, coal, and iron ore into the EEC, the United States, and Japan were to be successful (highly unlikely), the Chamber of Mines of South Africa and the Steel and Engineering Industries Federation of South Africa have estimated that a direct loss of 130,000 jobs (over 100,000 of them black jobs) could be expected. Whole towns, including Richards Bay, Saldanha Bay, Witbank, Middelburg, and Newcastle, would be gravely affected. The multiplier effects through the impact on the Electricity Supply Commission (ESCOM), South African Transport Services, and a range of other parastatal, private, and public companies could lead to a total loss of jobs conservatively estimated at about 300,000. In addition, if the dependents who rely on the salaries and wages of these workers are taken into account, those who would be seriously affected by these sanctions could number close to 2 million.

7. Increased Internecine Strife?

Since even mandatory UN sanctions are likely to be permeable, and the early phase of import substitution would stimulate the economy to some degree, some workers in the industries hit by sanctions would find new jobs elsewhere. But there would be significant regional imbalances within the country and these would contribute to existing tensions, heightening differences between the extremes in a polarized society and institutionalizing further bitterness.

Some of this anger would be directed at employers and the authorities, but increased internecine strife among labor and community leaders could also be expected. The net effect would be to perpetuate political, economic, and social fragmentation and to contribute to increased dissonance in industrial and community relations. Some of this is observable already, even within individual trade unions, as the prospect of job losses looms.

8. The Gold Caper

A multilateral attempt to drive down the price of gold, though given the imprimatur of *The Economist* (and, for a time, the U.S. Senate Foreign Relations Committee), is a nonstarter. There are far too many vested interests in the bullion trade, not the least of which are the expanding but highly price-vulnerable gold mining sectors of Australia, Canada, and the United States. Nor would the Soviet Union, in its current foreign-exchange-starved state, contemplate playing this card.

12

The 1987 Elections

Heribert Adam

June 1987

Of the 3 million white South Africans eligible to vote in the May 6, 1987 election, 67.97 percent cast ballots. At stake were 166 directly elected seats in the (white) House of Assembly of the country's tricameral parliament, plus 12 additional members nominated or indirectly elected in proportion to the parties' electoral strength. The National Party (which has held power since 1948) received 52.45 percent of the total votes cast and 133 seats (a gain of 6 seats), the Conservative Party 26.37 percent and 23 seats (a gain of 5), and the Herstigte Nasionale Party 3.14 percent (but lost its one parliamentary seat). Thus, the status quo and ultra-rightist parties took about 82 percent of the vote. As for the parties to the "left" of the NP, the Progressive Federal Party received 14.1 percent of the vote and 20 seats (a loss of 7 seats), the New Republic Party received 1.9 percent and 1 seat (a loss of 4), and three independents received 1.3 percent and 1 seat. In sum, the National Party was voted in by roughly 5 percent of the country's total population.

During the past few years, the white electorate has shifted in two contradictory ways: it moved to the left on apartheid issues but to the right on security. These shifts are not unrelated. The crumbling of certainty about traditional apartheid was a factor in bringing law and order issues to the fore. By cultivating (and also manufacturing) anxieties, the authorities lured doubting voters into their camp. By associating the PFP with the African National Congress, terrorism, and anarchy, the NP presented itself as the reliable guarantor of a basic human need.

Although no official tally is yet available, it is widely believed that, for the first time, the number of English-speaking whites voting for the National Party may have exceeded the number of Afrikaners. This new constituency of conservative "English" whites and immigrants is not perceptibly disturbed by the almost exclusive Afrikaner character of the party in terms of officeholders and imagery. On the contrary, Afrikaner nationalists are seen by the majority of English-speaking whites as the most trustworthy guardians of security. English support for the NP during the 1983 referendum on the new constitution was an endorsement of reform and power sharing; the 1987 support of the NP, on the other hand, was motivated by concern over "law and order."

In the past, Afrikaners supported the National Party because it was perceived as an emotional, ethnic home. This perception tended to generate a lifelong allegiance. The NP's new constituency of fearful English-speakers makes the party's support more volatile, more vulnerable to swings in the national mood, and more dependent on efficient media manipulation.

Another change dramatized in this election was that television has replaced the print media as the main communications weapon of the government. With the shift from concern for morality to strategies for maintaining control, television is the perfect manipulative tool. The state-owned South African Broadcasting Corporation (SABC) has excelled in its use of this new medium. It is ironical that the leadership of the National Party resisted the introduction of television until a decade ago, because of fears that it would undermine Afrikaner morale.

The right wing is difficult to categorize in class terms since ideological issues predominate. It is also noteworthy that the Conservative Party (founded under the leadership of Dr. Andries Treurnicht following the 1982 defection of 16 members of the NP parliamentary caucus in protest against the new constitutional proposals) achieved its gains without backing from either the SABC or any newspaper. Its campaign style reflected very much the National Party of earlier times.

One can say that the CP represents substantial sections of the Afrikaner lower middle class, of the urban and rural petty bourgeoisie, and of the employees of state enterprises. It absorbed what is left of the Afrikaner working class by virtually wiping out the rival HNP, and a right-wing white trade union leader (Arrie Paulus) was elected on a CP ticket. While the National Party has solidified its middle class support in both white ethnic groups, the CP's strength still lies more in rural areas and among the lower echelons of the civil service. Among the police, there is considerable sympathy for the extraparliamentary fascist Afrikaner Weerstandsbeweging (AWB) led by Eugene Terre' Blanche, which operates in loose alliance with the CP. The CP's strong showing is particularly significant in light of President P.W. Botha's sidetracking of reform, a preemptive move which, together with the declarations of emergencies, may have prevented an even greater electoral shift to the ultra-right.

Miscalculations on the Left

In terms of apartheid laws, the NP has moved into the realm that the Progressive Federal Party occupied in the past. The previous ideological currency of the PFP—negotiations, reform, and power sharing—has been taken over by the NP, while the CP now stands ideologically where the NP was five to 10 years ago. The PFP lost because it did not move farther to the left in response to this NP invasion but rather tried to compete with the NP on the same terrain.

The PFP-NRP alliance miscalculated the predilections of traditional NRP supporters, of whom at least 75 percent had already defected to the National Party when the alliance was formed. Some NRP supporters also still blamed the PFP for having destroyed the old United Party. Many voters on the left of the PFP deserted the party for its decision to remain in the tricameral white/Coloured/Indian parliament (established under the terms of the new constitution implemented in 1984) and for watering down its human rights principles by virtue of its pact with the more conservative NRP. This abstention lost the PFP marginal seats in university towns such as Pietermaritzburg and Grahamstown.

Meanwhile, elements of the upwardly mobile Afrikaner middle class deserted the NP to vote for former ambassador to Britain Denis Worrall and two other *verligte* members of the NP who left the party to run as independents in three key constituencies. These three wisely distanced themselves from overtures by the PFP, which was still tainted with an English-anti-Afrikaner-capitalist image, even for Afrikaner dissidents. In some ways, Worrall assumed the mantle of intellectual savior in the vacuum left by the resignation of Frederik van Zyl Slabbert as leader of the PFP and from parliament in February 1986. The independents did very well, winning one seat and suffering close defeats for the other two.

The liberal English-language press badly overestimated its influence as well as the appeal of the PFP-NRP alliance. By uncritically supporting the PFP and the independents to the hilt, the *Cape Times*, among others, lost credibility with both conservative and left-wing readerships. The crude attempts to create a bandwagon effect for the PFP and the independents backfired. The English papers generally failed to give adequate coverage of the extraparliamentary opposition as a new and separate force. Given the suspicion of things English that still exists in some traditionalist Afrikaner quarters, more nuanced press coverage of Worrall's candidacy might have helped him turn around the 39 votes by which he lost the Helderberg seat in Cape Province to Minister of Constitutional Development and Planning Chris Heunis.

The Omnipresent ANC

A major winner in the election was the banned African National Congress, which participated like a silenced phantom. Pretoria depicted the ANC as the major threat, both to National Party rule and the nation, thereby impeding attempts to create a credible middle ground. The increased presence of the ANC in South Africa now lies in its imposed absence. The more Pretoria criminalizes the movement, the more its symbolic appeal spreads. The election results represent a setback for Chief Buthelezi, who publicly endorsed the PFP-NRP platform.

The regime failed to take advantage of the opportunity to release Nelson Mandela (the life president of the ANC, imprisoned for over two decades) and other detainees at the very moment of triumph. Nobody could have accused P.W. Botha of weakness had he announced Mandela's unconditional release in his first postelection speech. This step would have offset the negative impression abroad of white voting behavior. Such an action, however, was ruled out by the demonization of the resistance movement in a campaign that further indoctrinated whites against compromises rather than preparing them for a negotiated settlement.

According to a number of surveys of whites, a majority feels that the government should negotiate with black leaders immediately and less than 10 percent of respondents are completely opposed to negotiations. However, 39 percent of those favoring negotiations have Buthelezi in mind, 10 percent say every black leader, and only 4 percent mention the ANC/Mandela. This clearly reflects the success of official indoctrination that the ANC are terrorists beyond the pale.

In the wake of the controversy over the alleged role of Chris Ball, managing director of First National (formerly Barclays) Bank, in placing an advertisement calling for the unbanning of the ANC, Pretoria has successfully cowed corporate heads into avoiding being labeled "friends of the enemy," at least for the time being. Business has largely failed to educate its own community for nonracial alternatives and negotiations outside government parameters. A conservative in-house constituency and lack of support among associates constrain even the handful of farsighted entrepreneurs. The "enemy-image" also harms profits when prejudiced customers and public institutions withhold orders or transfer their accounts.

NP Wins and Losses

The National Party caucus has been numerically strengthened, but weakened in its ideological cohesion. The party now lacks the previous solid endorsement of the Dutch Reformed Church, as well as the support of many of its intellectuals at the University of Stellenbosch and other key institutions. In this legitimation crisis, the NP government can be expected to rely increasingly on the security establishment and justify its rule in terms of maintaining law and order rather than moral claims or visions of an alternative. The loss of cohesion may trigger splits to both the left and right, dependent on dissatisfaction with the leadership and other issues.

The ultimate outcome of such a realignment in white politics would be two blocs: a right-wing party, comprising the CP and traditional Afrikaner nationalists in the NP, and a *verligte*/liberal bloc, comprising progressive Nats, independents, and the PFP. Unlike previous historical cleavages in white politics, this realignment would cut across ethnic lines. In the short run, however, patronage and power may temporarily reinforce the artificial NP unity.

One Possible Scenario

It is quite possible that the current three houses of parliament will neither be reelected nor have their terms extended in 1989, when new elections are due. The government, acting within the terms of the 1984 constitution, could find cause to suspend the legislative branch. Such a drastic step would be taken not because of a threat to the NP's parliamentary power from either the ultra-right or the liberals, but because of the politicizing upheaval that another attempted election of representatives to the "illegitimate" racially segregated houses of parliament would cause, particularly the (Coloured) House of Representatives and the (Indian) House of Delegates.

The democratic veneer for a pure executive state would be provided by periodic referenda on issues carefully selected and pretested. The new element of these plebiscites would most likely be a one-person-one-vote system that included all South African citizens, including blacks. The executive, endorsed by these referenda, would also be a multiracial one, including recognized black leaders willing to be co-opted. Important portfolios might be offered to a released Mandela, Buthelezi, and other credible opposition figures; this would probably be rejected by the ANC and United Democratic Front representatives but not necessarily by other black factions. Under such a nonracial system of periodic plebiscites, the government might hope to meet the demand for universal franchise on a common voters' roll ("broadening democracy"), regain some domestic and international legitimacy because of black inclusion and visibility on the executive ("highest level"), and still ensure "controlled and ordered change" under NP tutelage.

Resistance to a suspension of the present constitution would mainly come from the ultra-right. But since the Conservative Party has no chance of replacing the National Party at the polls, NP strategists would hope to pacify CP objections through patronage appointments in the expanded executive state. This would be marketed under the label of bringing together Afrikanerdom/whites and leaders of goodwill from other groups in an emergency coalition of all moderates.

It is possible that such an "interim government" might then seriously negotiate with the ANC. Since this government would be a nonracial executive with a broader base of conservatives from all groups, including business support, the ANC would probably not reject negotiations with such a formation. A straight seizure of power is now considered impossible by the majority of the ANC executive, including the South African Communist Party component of the leadership. Negotiations would be mainly about the terms of ANC inclusion and the restoration of a new parliamentary system rather than about the transfer of power.

Negotiations would not falter on the question of socialism and nationalization. The ANC, including the SACP, now advocates a mixed economy in which the major corporations would be taxed rather than taken over. But in four areas a substantial restructuring of existing economic relations could be expected —(1) a redistribution of underutilized land to African farmers, (2) a far-reaching industrial democracy with statutory union participation in major management decisions along the lines of the German codetermination model, (3) a rapid Africanization of the civil service, particularly the parastatals, and (4) a nationalization of banks, as in France. A reformed social-democratic welfare capitalism could reach an acceptable compromise with the ANC on all four issues.

Prospects for the Near Term

Despite a simmering civil war, the majority of whites do not yet perceive the situation in South Africa as at a crisis stage. Sanctions remain symbolic and have not really hurt so far. The 50 percent decline in the value of the currency since 1985 has benefited the export sector. The Johannesburg stock market is booming as never before, and the dollar price of gold has risen significantly. Cash-saturated local conglomerates are happy to buy out disinvesting foreign companies at bargain prices. Few politicians and privileged voters focus on the long-term costs of a delegitimated state with a siege economy; instead, they are lulled by the short-term boom of import substitution and inflation. The growing structural unemployment and soaring crime rate have not yet made life intolerable in the secluded white enclaves of affluence.

In sum, the political crisis in South Africa will worsen before it gets better. Only when a shared perception of stalemate exists will both sides negotiate in good faith. As long as each side feels in the ascendancy, the violence without victory will continue.

Index

Abrahams, Lionel, 172

Adam, Heribert, 104–126, 183–191

African National Congress (ANC), 36–40; business leaders and, 121–122; Communism and, 16, 54, 117, 122–124; destabilization policy and, 90; Front Line states and, 108, 117, 123; future of, 102; guerrilla tactics, 149–150; history and philosophy of, 36–37; InKatha and, 45; new constitution and, 119; 1987 elections and, 187–188; Nkomati Pact and, 91, 93, 117; nonviolence and, 102, 122–124; popularity of, 5–6, 168; reemergence of, 139–140; regional detente and, 105; revolution and 150–151; South Africa and, 87–88, 103, 120–126, 176–177, 189–190; Soviet arms and, 118; UDF and, 120, 142–143; Zimbabwe and, 94

Africans. *See* Black politics; specific groups, nations

Afrikaner Weerstandsbeweging (AWB), 185

Afrikaners: demographic changes, 2; politics of. *See* South African government

Aggett, Neil, 146

Alexander, Neville, 50, 82

ANC. *See* African National Congress

Angola: apartheid and, 106, 110; MPLA, 96, 108–109; recent developments in, 88; South Africa and, 87, 89, 95–100; Soviet Union and, 98–99

Apartheid policy: Angola and, 106, 110; capitalism and, 109–110; Front Line states and, 110, 118–119; future of, 127–138; loss of hegemony, 17; Mozambique and, 93; new constitution and, 103, 119; opposition politics, 118–120; quality of black education and, 60–62; sanctions and, 118–119, 175–191; S. A. government attitude and, 7, 127; technocratic rule and, 10 UDF and, 50; Western aid and, 115–116; white electorate and, 183; Zimbabwe and, 94

Asian(s): political rights of, 66,